May-Britt

My Life's Journey

May-Britt

My Life's Journey

by
May-Britt Pedersen

as told to LaVonne Quinth

Illustrations by Jeremy Grant

MAY-BRITT MY LIFE'S JOURNEY

Copyright ©2009 May-Britt Pedersen
ISBN 978-0-578-02235-2

Written by LaVonne Quinth
Edited by Carol Norheim Carlson
Ilustrations by Jeremy Grant
Graphic design by LaVonne Quinth

Scripture taken from:
HOLY BIBLE, NEW INTERNATIONAL VERSION®. NIV®.
Copyright© 1973, 1978, 1984 by International Bible Society.
Used by permission of Zondervan. All rights reserved.

PRINTED IN THE UNITED STATES OF AMERICA

Blessed are those whose strength is in you,
who have set their hearts on pilgrimage.

As they pass through the Valley of Baca,
they make it a place of springs;
the autumn rains also cover it with pools.

They go from strength to strength,
till each appears before God in Zion.

Psalms 84:5-7

*A*s I go into the sunset of my life, I have decided to share my life story with the people that I love most.

Orla, for fifty years you have stood by me in the sunshine and in the rain in my life, in sickness and in health. When I was hospitalized in 2004 for heart trouble and was given a pacemaker, I was weak, sick and terrified. You were my rock and my comforter. You were patient and loving, even when I ruined our trip to Arizona with my tears and frustrations. I will never forget how you took care of me. As we grow older together, I know that you will always be by my side. I love you.

LaVonne, you came into my life in 1961. It has been a joy to raise you up to the woman you are today. You were the compliant child, always fun, happy most of the time.

Orla Jens, I didn't think I could love anyone as much as I loved LaVonne, but then you came along in 1964, and oh…. I was so happy! I loved you so much, and I still do. What a joy it was to raise you and to see the person you have become.

I thank my God for seven magnificent grandchildren, each unique in personality, each truly a Divine Gift.

Jonathan, your name means *Gift of the Lord*, which proved to be true. We were so excited about our first grandson, and throughout the years you have been a joy to me. I love when you sing and play the guitar. It was a very special day for me, as I know it was for you, when you followed the Lord in baptism.

Erik, your name means *Brave and Honored One*. You were such an easy baby. I remember when you could just sit up, if you fell over you would just get back up again without ever crying. What I really remember about you is that when you got a little older you were always looking out for your younger siblings. Your gentleness, helpfulness and caring has been a beautiful thing to see.

Nicolas, your name means *Victorious and Triumphant*. You were such a happy baby growing up. Even when you had to sit in time out, you just decided to be happy. When you were six years old you got chickens for your birthday. The deal was that if you took care of them, you could do anything you wanted with the money for the first sale of eggs. So, of course, you bought candy and ate it all at once. I was in the kitchen when you came running, throwing up all the way to the bathroom. I said, "Nicolas! You ate too much candy." You answered, "I know. I made too much money."

Stephanie, your name means *Illuminated*. How you live up to that name. You have brought so much joy to me. You are so beautiful, smart and you say the funniest things. One day you came home from school after having a lesson in sex education. You walked in the door and exclaimed, "Now I know why Uncle Jens and Aunt Darla adopted their kids. They didn't want to do that yucky stuff!!"

Oliver, your name means *Kind and Affectionate, Bringer of Peace*. I'm so glad you are here, the only blond kid in the family. I was privileged to be there when you were only a month old. It was in the middle of winter and your mom did not feel real well, but you brought light and smiles to all of us.

Lydia, your name means *Beautiful Light, Lover of the Lord*. It was a special day when you came into our family and you are a very special girl. I have never known anyone who talked as early as you did. We had a lot of fun. One time when I was taking care of you while your parents were away, we had a special time of bonding. I loved taking care of you.

Mallory, your name means *Joyful, Counselor*. What a joy you are, so beautiful with brown eyes and the same complexion as your sister. Sometimes we walked with the stroller on the street in front of my house and on the way back we stopped to pick some flowers. What beautiful memories I have of the time I've spent with you.

You have all shared my life and made it meaningful and joyous. Now I would like to share with you my memories, the joys and the sorrow, good times and bad times, and the events and people who have shaped my life.

May-Britt

My Parents
and Grandparents

Samuel and Anna

I remember my grandfather, my father's father, Samuel Jonasson, as a very kind and gentle man. He was a little man, not very tall, but tough and hard working, and always very healthy.

For his 90th birthday a newspaper reporter came to the village to interview him. Arriving in the village he saw a man bring a large milk jug down to the road on a bicycle, effortlessly swinging it up onto the milk platform. He thought the man looked to be early middle-aged, and stopped to ask directions.

"There is supposed to be an old man in this area who is turning 90 on Sunday, would you know where he lives?"

Samuel raised himself to his full stature and replied, "Well, that would probably be me!" Bringing the reporter into the farmhouse kitchen, he told him his story. This is from the articles that appeared in the local newspaper.

That was my first meeting with the 90-year-old railroad worker, American traveler and Småland farmer, a sturdy Samuel Jonasson from Ryd. After a lifetime of breaking up the rocky soil and removing huge rocks from the fields on his farm in Ryd, he handles the heavy milk jug with ease. With his enormous energy and vigor he seems to be barely past his 30's.

Having met other vigorous and healthy 85+ year olds and described them as "incredibly spry" or a "young 90 year old," I find myself at a loss for words to describe Samuel Jonassson. Perhaps it is enough to say that he spent his 89th summer digging up large rocks from his fields with an iron bar.

Hard work is good for you, says the honorable old man and is a little disgruntled with his family who would rather he slowed down a bit. After eight decades of working hard morning to evening it is impossible to just sit around and do nothing.

Samuel was born in Ryd in 1858. He was one of seven children. Times were hard and the family was poor. He was 10 years old in 1868 when crops failed all over Sweden. "Actually," he said, "the following year was the hardest when we had to live on the little we had harvested the year before." To stretch the precious flour, people ground up bark or straw and added to the bread. Bark bread was not very tasty, he recalls.

Småland is a rock-strewn landscape, and the area where my Grandparents lived was one of the rockiest areas in all of Småland. To clear the fields they had to dig up all the rocks and move them out of the way. If the rock was too big to move they planted around it. Sometimes they used dynamite on the rocks. They used the rocks from the fields to build stone walls. In his lifetime my grandfather probably built more stone walls then anyone in the area. If you visit Ryd you'll see long stone walls running across the landscape; my grandfather built many of them.

When he was 14 he and a few friends headed north to work on the railroad that was being built in northern Sweden. He was diligent and hard working and soon became a foreman. Being from Småland he was used to digging up rocks, moving rocks and building with rocks and so this became his specialty. Whenever a stone bridge needed to be constructed they would call on Samuel Jonasson.

After six years of working on the railroad Samuel returned home. He worked on his father's farm for three or four years then, yearning for adventure, set off for America. In northern Michigan his special talents were a welcome asset. He got a job building the railroad making better money then ever before. But his heart just wasn't in it and his time in the U.S. was short lived. "You see, I had met Anna, that's my old lady, see, and even if I made lots of money she was the reason I bought a ticket home."

My grandmother Anna was born in 1871, the eldest of seven children. She was also interviewed when she turned 90 but had only a few memories from her childhood. She said the memories come back when she lay in bed at night and pulled the covers over her head. One of her more vivid memories was when, as a young girl, they were moving from one farm to another. Although still very young, she drove the moving wagon pulled by two oxen. The heavy load shifted and the wagon tipped. There she sat waiting for help to arrive. She also spoke of the year her father was sick and she ran the farm all by herself.

I remember my grandmother was much bigger and taller than my grandfather. I think she was the more domineering of the two, but was also often cheerful and jovial. I remember how her ample stomach jiggled up and down when she laughed. She had problems with high blood pressure and swollen legs, and would use leaches to bring down the swelling. Placing them on her legs, they would suck out the blood until they were big and fat.

Then she would squeeze the blood out of them and use them again. Of course she could only do this a few times before the leeches died and she would need new leeches.

We had bloodsucker leeches in Ljungsjön, one of the lakes on our farm. I'd heard that she needed new leaches, so I went down to the lake equipped with a bottle and a stick. I could have picked them up with my fingers but they would grab on right away and start sucking blood, so I decided it was best to use a stick. It was easy and there were plenty of them. Bloodsuckers are about 3-4 inches long with brown stripes on their back. There were other leeches in the lake that were about the same size and shape, but were solid black. It was important to know the difference. The black ones didn't suck blood.

I collected eight or ten leeches, put them in the bottle and filled it with water. I put a cloth over the top and tied it with a string so they couldn't get out but would still have oxygen. I placed the bottle in my backpack and bicycled up to Ryd, about 10 kilometers. My grandmother was pleased to get the new leeches.

Samuel and Anna were married in 1889. With the money he had made in America they were able to buy a small farm in Eskekärr where five of their six children were born. Sometime around the turn of the century they bought the farm in Lindö where I would later be born. In 1920 they sold Lindö to my father and moved back to Ryd where they lived until they died. They both lived to be over 90 years old, maybe bark bread is good for you after all!

Religion and faith was very personal for both Samuel and Anna. They rarely spoke of their

Farfar and Farmor
My father's parents

Samuel Jonasson was born in Ryd in 1860. He visited the USA when he was young but returned to Sweden to marry Anna. He died in 1951.

He had six siblings, but I only know the names of three:

Per-Johan lived in Sweden with his family

Anders lived in Sweden and had several children.

Tilda had one son named Gustav

Anna was born in Draget 1871, she died in 1963.

She was the oldest of seven children, but I only know about one of them.

Oskar lived in Sweden and had many children.

Samuel and Anna were married and set up housekeeping in Eskekärr where a most of their children were born. Around the turn of the century they bought a small farm called Lindö. Later they sold it to their son Gunnar and moved back to Ryd.

faith or went to church, but all of their children were baptized and confirmed in the Lutheran Church. My grandfather read his Bible every day. When asked how much of it he had read he said, "Well, from cover to cover ten times, and besides that a lot more in between." When asked what advice he would give young people he said, " Read the Bible. There is a lot of good advice in that book."

All noble families have at least one skeleton in the closet!

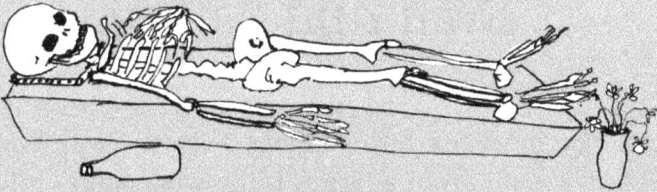

Samuel's brother, Anders, had a daughter, Stefany, who had a son that was called "Paul from Hult." He disappeared without a trace in 1985, have turned off the electricity, cleaned and closed up his house, and paid all of his bills. Fifteen years later, when the forest was being cleared, a large mound was found not far from his home. They discovered an entrance, now nearly undetectable under all the moss and bushes. Upon entering they found a small room with a bed in the corner. A wall vase, with flowers now dead and dry, had fallen off the wall. The skeleton of a man was found lying on a mattress, a bottle of soda and a small gas lamp nearby. Apparently Paul, for it was him they found, had carefully constructed his own tomb, taken care of his worldly affairs and then retired to this lonely room to die.

Sven and Jenny

$\mathcal{M}$y mother's father, Sven Nilsson, was born in 1880. He came from a large family with eight children. As a young man he made plans to immigrate to America together with six of his siblings. But then he met Jenny. His brothers and sister set off for a new land and he stayed at home and married the woman he loved.

They lived in Klerebo where they owned a small farm located near the state church where Sven was the bell ringer. He rang the bells for every service, every funeral, every wedding, and also every Saturday evening at 6 PM to ring in the day of rest. When someone in the community died, he rang the bells. They called that "ringing them into heaven."

The bell tower in the church in Hjälmseryd was very high and he had to walk up many steps. As his grandchildren we were allowed to come up with him and watch. The bells, three of them, were rung with separate foot pumps, and required three men. Sven was in charge, and rang the largest bell. It had to be carefully synchronized and was very interesting to watch.

He started ringing the bells in 1914. By the time he turned 70 he had rung the bells 7000 times and was awarded a gold medal from the Bishop for 36 years of faithful service.

He attended church every Sunday, always sitting three rows from the front on the right side. He took his hat off when he came in, and when he sat down in the pew he would put his face in the hat and pray.

Sven was also the community butcher. Few of the farmers knew how to butcher a pig, so they would ask Sven. He came on his bike with his tools to any farmer who needed him. He helped the farmers with other things too. If a cow had a problem delivering her calf, he would come out and help with that also. My dad knew how to butcher, so we seldom needed to call on my Grandfather for help with our animals.

He was a proud man and always told us to walk straight like you are proud of yourself. He did that himself. According to him there was nothing he couldn't do! He often bragged about fights he'd had in his younger days. He was left-handed, and he would always surprise them with a hard left hook.

He was a good man, very religious and faithful in attending the state church. He was also very generous. When the little Pentecostal group decided to build a chapel, he donated the land, even though he was never involved in the Pentecostal Church himself.

He was domineering at home, and his decisions were final. Jenny didn't have much to say. Although he was active in the community and involved in many things, his wife never went anywhere.

Morfar
My mother's father

Sven Nilsson was born in Draget in 1880. His parents came from Kronobergs län, which is the southern part of Sweden around the city of Växsjö. He was preparing to travel to the USA with his siblings when he met Jenny, and instead stayed in Sweden to marry her. He died in 1969.

He had four brothers and two sisters:

August immigrated to the USA but returned to Sweden when he contracted Tuberculosis. He married and settled in Klerebo. He had five children.

Salomon immigrated to the USA, married and settled in California. He had two daughters.

Daniel immigrated to the USA. He was killed in a train accident.

Claes immigrated to the USA. He was killed in a construction accident.

Ester immigrated to the USA, married and settled in Denver. She had 13 children.

Tilda married and lived in Linnevik. She had five children.

Mormor
My mother's mother

Jenny was born in Axaryd in 1881. She was working for her uncle, the farmer in Grönvik, when she met Sven who was probably working as a farmhand. She died in 1961.

She had two brothers and two sisters:

Gustav traveled to the USA five different times, even experiencing the great earthquake of 1906 in San Francisco. He eventually decided to live in Sweden. He lived until he was 90 years old and died in the convalescent home in Hjälmseryd.

Claes immigrated to the USA.

Emma immigrated to the USA where she settled in Montana. She had four children.

Beda immigrated to the USA.

Sven and Jenny were married and settled in Klerebo, on the farm that is farthest up the road. They later moved to Brohult, but when their home burnt down in 1919 they moved back to Klerebo, this time to the first farm on the road.

My grandmother, Jenny, was born in 1881. I remember her always working and talking to herself. You always knew what she was thinking because she would say it out loud. If a pot boiled over on the stove she would get upset and swear at it. Contrary to my grandfather who always walked straight and tall, Jenny's back was crooked and bent. She was always carrying things to and from the barn. When she had milked and fed the cows, she carried in the milk into the house. After separating the cream from the milk, she carried the skim milk back out to the barn to feed the calves and pigs. Carrying in water and wood was also her job.

My grandmother was always interested in world events and in politics. Since she was always talking to herself we knew her views. While Jenny leaned toward the conservative parties, my grandfather was more liberal. Since she never left the house, not even to vote, he would take both his and her ballots to the election hall and vote for both of them. That way he doubled his vote.

As kids we always enjoyed going to Klerebo. My grandparents were kind to us and we always felt welcome. They lived in Klerebo until they died, my grandmother in 1961 at the age of 80, and my grandfather in 1969, at the age of 89.

Gunnar and Ester

My father, Gunnar, was born in Eskeskär in 1897 as one of six children. When he was still very young the family moved to the farm in Lindö, where he grew up. My father lived a life full of hard work, many sorrows and many joys. I remember him often quoting the scripture:

Sons are a heritage from the Lord
children a reward from him.
Psalms 127:3

And he was rewarded with seven children! He was very strict and when he told us something, we did not argue about it, we just obeyed. We had more fun when he was not in the house. Of course, when he was out working in the fields we often had to be there too, to help out. He didn't communicate very well, was quicker to hit than to explain, but there was also a gentle and good side to him. It just didn't show up as often.

13

He was a very hard-working man doing everything on the farm that the women couldn't do. After a hard days work in the fields, he would come in and eat dinner and then lay down on the sofa to rest. It was different for my mother. After working hard in the fields, she had chores to do in the barn, milking the cows and feeding the animals. Then she came inside and had to make dinner and after dinner there was always something that needed doing. A woman's work was never finished, but the men had time to rest.

Hunting was my father's favorite pastime, and sometimes it got him into trouble. One day two swans landed on Göla. It was too great a temptation. He went out and shot them, knowing that it was illegal but, after all, it was his own lake. Somebody notified the police and they came out to give him a fine. Gossip flew around the neighborhood, "Gunnar shot the swans! He belongs to the Pentecostal church and they are supposed to be so holy!" We were all embarrassed. In church on Sunday he stood up and confessed what he had done and asked forgiveness. He grew about ten feet in my eyes that day.

During the war years, 1939 to 1945, gasoline was not available. A few cars and buses that ran on wood burners could still be used, but there were otherwise very few cars around. As soon as the war was over, Dad went out and bought a used car, an Opal Regent. It was delivered to the farm and, although he had no idea how to drive it, he couldn't leave it alone. He took it for a drive on the little road from Lindö. Keeping it in first gear, he controlled the speed with the clutch. It smoked like crazy! Once out on the main road he turned around. Someone who knew how to drive stopped and showed him how to put it in neutral and how to change gears. He later went to driving school and eventually got his license, but he was never a good driver. It's a wonder that he didn't have any accidents; of course there was very little traffic. If he did come into the city where the traffic was heavier, he would wait for a while at an

intersection then, tired of waiting, he would say, "Now it's my turn!" and he would go!

In 1920 my grandparents bought a farm in Ryd and my father bought the farm in Lindö from them. In 1928 he married my mother and brought her to live on the farm.

My mother, Ester, was born in Klerebo in 1906. She loved Klerebo with its rolling hills and cherry orchards, and would bicycle down to see her mother whenever she had a chance, which wasn't very often. She felt that Lindö was so far away and often complained that it was at the end of the world.

I don't know how my parents met. They didn't speak about such things, but I know that she was very proud of him and thought that he was so handsome. I also know that they were crazy about sex! I know this because on several occasions Linnea and I spied on them! One morning I came down to the kitchen early. My mother quickly got up off the sofa where my father lay, straightened her clothes and quickly began preparing breakfast, muttering to herself, "Now how am I going to get through this day without having gotten any of that?"

My mother gave birth to eight children and had at least two miscarriages. It seemed to me that she was always either pregnant or had just had a baby. She was such a wonderful person, so kind and always wanting the best for us. Although she sometimes pinched or pulled our hair if we were naughty, we knew that she would never spank us. My father was the disciplinarian and would be the one to spank us, often, whether we needed it or not. My mother suffered with us when he spanked us. Like her mother, she would talk to herself and we could hear her reasoning, "If I tell him what they did, then he will spank them too hard." So she didn't always tell our father of all our wrong doings.

Mamma and I

She was a spunky woman who rode a small motorcycle to Lamhult, a nearby town, something unheard of for women in that day. She wrote editorials to the newspaper about things she considered to be social injustices. For example, she felt that, compared to city women, farm women were treated poorly when they went to the hospital to have their babies.

One day when my father had gone to the mill she looked out and saw a wild rabbit in the yard. She went in and got my father's gun and shot it. Somehow word got out that Ester had shot a rabbit in her yard. Someone reported it to the police and they came out to give her a fine because she didn't have a license to use the gun. Tough as she was, she sat down and wrote a letter to His Majesty the King of Sweden. She told him that she did not deserve a fine. All she did was shoot a rabbit on her own farm, using her husband's gun. She received an answer from the King pardoning her. I wish I had that letter. Unfortunately we do not have it, or the letters she wrote to the newspaper.

In addition to all the pregnancies and miscarriages, my mother was often ill. I remember when she had a sinus infection. She had to flush out her sinuses with a big hook, which she inserted up her nose. It had a pump on it and she used it several times a day. Eventually she got better, but I think I prefer the antibiotics we have today! Sick or well, life continues on the farm and she had to do a lot of work even when she wasn't feeling well, but it was very difficult for me to see her sick so often.

She also suffered from stomach troubles. In 1951 the doctors scheduled her for ulcer surgery but when they opened her up they discovered she had gallstones, and decided to remove them first. She must have been in terrible pain.

My father was also sick and hospitalized at the time. He lost a lot of weight and was so extremely fatigued that he could barely walk. After many tests it was determined that his adrenal glands were not producing the hormones he needed. He had been repeatedly hospitalized during the preceding year and, at the time of my mother's surgery, was in the same hospital.

Mother didn't recover well from the gallbladder surgery and she was dying. They brought my father in to her bedside when I was in her room. He bent over her and said, "I have not always understood you. Would you forgive me?" She answered, "We will have to forgive each other." A few hours later she uttered her final words, "Now I see Jesus."

She died in November 1951 at 45 years of age, leaving my father with six children still at home; Kurt, the youngest, was only eight months old. Father eventually recovered from his illness, but it took a long time. He came home to Lindö where he lived until 1958 when the house burned down. Although he continued to farm the land he never rebuilt the house, saying that the place held too many bad memories. He moved closer to Hjälmseryd and then finally to Klerebo where he lived the rest of his life.

Father came to visit us in America in 1966. My sister, Solveig, and I were both living in California with our families, and my youngest sister, Yvonne, was in Los Angeles working as an au pair. By this time Father had regained his strength and was healthy and vibrant. He claimed that he had been healed.

He and Orla got along really well. Orla taught him to paint and took him with him on the job. He stayed with us from September to March, enjoying a California winter, before returning to Sweden in the spring.

In 1976 he suffered a stroke and died two weeks later. He was 78. I went home for his funeral and we buried him next to my mother.

There had never been a gravestone over my mother's grave, but after my father died we had one made with both their names. Whenever I go back to Hjälmseryd I always visit their graves and remember them.

Father

Gunnar Samuelsson was born in Eskeskärr, Sweden in 1897. He went to school in Karshult. There is a photograph of him and his siblings hanging in the old school house which is now a museum. He died in 1976 after suffering a stroke.

He had five siblings:

Oskar immigrated to the USA when he was 17. He was married twice, and lived in Chicago until he retired and moved to Florida.

Emily married in Sweden and had eight children.

Viktoria married in Sweden and had eight children.

Gerda married in Sweden and had three children.

Rut married in Sweden and had four children.

Mother

Esther was born in 1906 in Klerebo. She went to school and was confirmed in Hjälmseryd. She married Gunnar in 1928 and moved to his farm in Lindö. She died in 1951 from complications following gallbladder surgery.

She had three siblings.

Gustav lived in Hjämseryd, was never married but had one daughter.

Bertha was married and lived in Hundåsen. She had one son.

Simon never married, he inherited the farm in Klerebo and lived there until he moved to a nursing home.

Gunnar and Esther were married in 1928 in Hjälmseryd's church. They lived on the farm in Lindö and had eight children, Linnea, May-Britt, Åke (died when he was two years old), Birgitta, Solveig, Ove, Yvonne, and Kurt

My Siblings

1953

Linnea was born in 1928. She married Helge Hjertonsson and they live in Hjälmseryd. They have two children. Els-Marie and Roger, seven grandchildren, and seven great-grandchildren. (and still counting)

Birgitta was born in 1937. She married Erik Nilsson and they live in Årjäng. They have six children, Kristina, Anne-Marie, Sven, Olle, Per and Lisa, and nine grandchildren.

Solveig was born in 1939. She immigrated to the USA in 1956. She has four sons, Dwight, Duane, David and Donald, and nine grandchildren, so far.

My Siblings

2000

Ove was born in 1943. He married Ingalill and together they immigrated to the USA in 1970. They have three daughters, Anna, Ingela and Jennifer, and four grandchildren.

Yvonne was born in 1946. She married Bengt Maars and they live in Vrigstad. They have five children, Magnus, Linda, Martin, Marcus and Morton. They have six grandchildren so far.

Kurt was born in 1951. He is now married to Lena and they live in Vrigstad.

There are so many things I wish I had asked my parents and my grandparents, but I didn't think about it until it was too late. That is why I am writing all of this down, I would like to share the things I remember about my life.

Growing Up

My Early Years

I was born on August 31, 1932, right there in the living room of our farmhouse. I was brought into the world by a midwife, who had arrived late but still in time to help my mother. They say I was born on the day they finished the harvest that year. My sister, Linnea, was four years old when I was born.

In Sweden at that time the children's last name was derived from their father's first name. Gunnar was Samuel's son so his last name was Samuelsson. They didn't make a distinction between sons and daughters though, so since my father's name was Gunnar my last name was Gunnarsson.

Åke

When I was just one year old my little brother, Åke, was born. We became the best of friends. I'm amazed how many things I remember from him. We were always playing together.

One time we went into the chicken coop and started breaking the eggs. We climbed up into the hen's nests and took one egg at a time and threw them on a rock; it was so much fun to see the eggs break. Porcelain eggs were sometime placed in the nests to entice the hen's to lay eggs. When we came across a porcelain egg we tried and tried, but we couldn't break it. We kept trying but said, "It's just impossible." My father came in, and we thought we were in big trouble. But I think he found the situation so comical, watching us trying to break that porcelain egg, he just picked us up and brought us in to mother and told her the story.

It's funny the things you remember. One day my father was sitting under a tree in our front yard; I was probably three years old at the time. Åke and I were playing nearby. Whatever we did, we did it together. Our neighbor came over and my father asked him, "Have you seen my twins?"

One day we were working on "Mossen," a field that was located about 800 meters up the road towards Ljungsjön. Åke decided to go home, but he missed Lindö and continued through the forest and ended up in Karshult, three kilometers away. We have often wondered how a 2 year old could walk that far, over rocks and through the forests, crossing several small creeks.

This picture, taken on his christening day, is the only picture I have of Åke. Mother is holding him and I am the little girl in the foreground looking back My father looks so happy and proud of his little family.

25

I remember the panic when they realized that he was gone. My mother, after exhausting every place to look, was lying in the grass crying. She saw a vision of a cross in the grass. I don't know how she interpreted that, if it was a comfort or a warning, but miraculously, Bertil, a man from Karshult, came up the road with Åke on his shoulders. He had found him on his farm, probably fast asleep. There were no telephones in those days, so Bertil had to guess where this child belonged. I have such a clear memory of them coming over the little hill at the south end of the farm, Åke riding on Bertil's shoulders with a little red bag of cookies in his hand. Oh what joy there was in our family!

Later that summer Åke wandered away again and disappeared. This time Bertil didn't bring him back on his shoulders. Neighbors and relatives were contacted, and they formed a "skallgång" or a search team that scoured the countryside. I think they searched for two days. He was finally found, drowned in a deep hole between Göla and the house. I remember they placed his body on a table in the barn. His little hands were all clinched together. My memories are so vivid. I was only three years old, but I had lost my best friend, and I didn't understand.

I also remember his funeral. There were a lot of people around and a lot of beautiful flowers. I had a bouquet of flowers that I held tightly in my hand. I thought they were the prettiest flowers I had ever seen. At the cemetery my father took my hand and told me to throw the flowers into this big hole. I didn't understand what that hole was. I thought it might be a well. We had wells on the farm, but I had never seen a grave. I couldn't understand why he wanted me to throw those beautiful flowers into the well. He had to pry my fingers open. I remember thinking it was dumb to throw them away, and I decided that next time I had flowers I would hold on to them no matter what.

What are the chances?

Fifty-four years later, Linnea's son-in-law, Arne, was remodeling an old house in Släthult. Tearing the walls apart he came across some old newspapers that had been used as insulation. Curious about what may have been written so many years ago he glanced through the pages and his eyes caught on a small announcement about the funeral of a young boy. He brought the article to Linnea and she confirmed that it was about Åke, our little brother.

Spectacular serendipity! What are the chances that that newspaper clipping would be found by someone in our family after hanging inside those walls for over 50 years? And what are the chances that Arne would decide to look at that particular page among all the pages he was tearing down? It blows my mind but I am so grateful. I have that clipping tucked away with other memories of my childhood.

Here is the clipping that was miraculously found inside the walls of a house that was being renovated.

— Annandag pingst jordfästes stoftet efter den genom olyckshändelse omkomne gossen Kurt Ake Gunnarsson från Lindö. Efter det "Tryggare kan ingen vara" sjungits, förrättades jordfästningen av pastor Landervik, som även talade känsligt och varmt till de sörjande. Efter en sång talade sedan John Stork från Skärshult. En myckenhet av blommor ägnades den lilles minne. *⅟₆ –36*

The remains of the young boy, Kurt Åke Gunnarsson from Lindö, whose death was accidental, were buried on the second day of Easter (Monday.) After the congregation sang "Tryggare kan ingen vara" (Children of the Heavenly Father) Pastor Landervik conducted the funeral speaking warmly and sensitively to the mourners. Another song was sung and then John Stork, from Skärshult, spoke. An abundance of flowers were laid on the grave in memory of the little boy.

June 1, 1936

Standing in front of our house in Lindö. From left to right: Linnea, Aunt Berta, me, mother holding Ove. In front of us is Solveig and Birgitta.

Birgitta

Birgitta was born in 1937. They decided that mother wouldn't have the baby at home this time; she would go to the hospital. Unfortunately Birgitta was in a hurry. They had only come half way to Jönköping when she was born in the car.

Mother was always worried about Birgitta. She was so skinny and she'd already had pneumonia twice. One day early in the spring, Linnea and I were going for a walk and we asked if we could take Birgitta with us. Mother agreed but told us to be very careful with her and not let her get cold. We walked down the road and across the marshlands until we came to a ditch filled with water. Linnea and I could easily jump over it, but what should we do with Birgitta? We decided that Linnea would stand on one side and catch her when I threw her over. But just as I was going to throw her to the other side, Birgitta got scared and grabbed on to me, and I dropped her in the ditch. We fished her up and took her straight home to mother. Acting as heros, we told her that Birgitta had fallen into a ditch and we had rescued her.

She was a pretty tough girl, though. When she was five years old she wanted to build a wagon. She found a board and was trying to cut it into pieces with an ax when she missed, and cut off her middle toe. It is a mystery how she could manage to cut off her middle toe without damaging any of the others! They took her to the hospital in Värnamo, 40 kilometers away. It was very upsetting and I cried.

Solveig and Ove

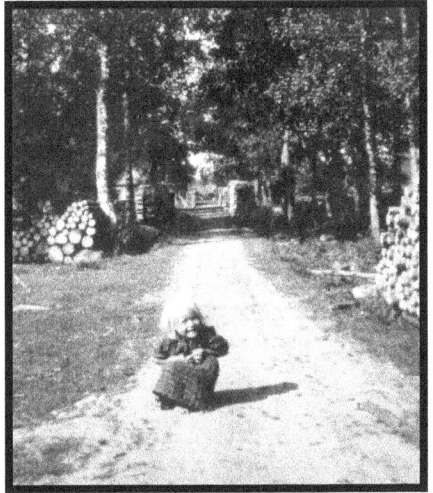

Solveig was born in 1939, but I have no memories of her arrival. I do have vague memories from 1943 when my brother, Ove, was born. I remember my mother coming home with a baby boy. They were so happy to have a boy again, my father whistled as he worked in the fields.

When Ove was a young boy he was playing on a large pile of logs stacked about six feet high. My father was working nearby. Ove was running back and forth

Solveig sitting on the road to Lindö.

on the logs when one of them slipped. He fell, the loose log coming down on top of him hitting him in the eye. Father carried him, bloody and screaming, into Mother. "Here is your son," he said.

They took him to the hospital in Värnamo where they were able to save the eye, but his vision was permanently damaged.

Linnea is Hospitalized

When I was nine years old Linnea and I were walking home from Hultet, which is on the other side of Ljungsjön. It is a long walk, about 3-4 kilometers. Linnea started to get very sick with a high fever, and was so tired she could barely walk home. It turned out that she had scarlet fever. My father rode his bicycle four or five kilometers to Slättö to the nearest telephone and called the ambulance. She was in the hospital in isolation for six weeks. I remember I was so jealous that she got to ride in the ambulance and then stay at the hospital. She wrote some letters to us at home and told us how nice it was. They had indoor toilets! That was something she had never seen before. She told me later that the first time she used the toilet, she pulled the chain and it made the most horrible noise. She thought the whole hospital was going to collapse!

Bashful

I was painfully shy; I wouldn't talk to anyone or even answer when they talked to me. Kristin, a lady who lived at the end of Ljungsjön, thought that I was deaf and dumb.

One day when I was eight or nine years old my father asked me to go up to our neighbors in Kroxhylte and pick up the newspaper. Newspapers were delivered to the mailman in Skärshult, which was about two miles away. Our neighbors picked up our paper along with their own; that way we only had to walk a mile to their house to get it. This was the first time he asked me to go and get the paper. It was the middle of winter and already dark. I was scared, but I knew that I had to do as I was told.

Lake Göla was frozen so I took the shortcut over the ice. I wasn't afraid of crossing the ice, I knew it would hold, but the forest was dark and scary. I saw a moose lying by the side of the road. His head was shaking, and I have always wondered if he was shaking it at me or if I was the one that was shaking. It was so frightening. To this day I don't like to walk past that spot alone.

Finally I got to the house in Kroxhylte. I stood there, just inside the door, too bashful to speak. They knew I was there to get the newspaper, but I think they wanted to see how long I would stand there without talking. I don't know how long I stood there, but the longer it took, the longer it would be before I would have to go back through the forest and past that moose. Finally they got tired of waiting for me to say something, and gave me the paper. I left without ever saying a word.

All the way home I kept thinking about that moose. I was so frightened I was shaking all over. At home they had begun to worry, and sent Linnea out to look for me. She met me on the ice out in the middle of the lake. I'll never forget how happy I was to see her, to see someone I wasn't afraid to talk to. I told her all about the shaking moose.

New Dress

Every spring I would get a new dress. Mother bought the material and I would bicycle the 12 kilometers to the seamstress in Rörvik. Jenny Sjödal took my measurements, talking continually. I, of course, didn't say a thing. A couple of weeks later I would bicycle back for a fitting. Then, after a couple more weeks, I would bicycle and pick up my dress. I was so excited about getting a new dress that bicycling all that way three times didn't bother me at all. In Sweden they say, "He who waits for a good thing, never waits too long."

> *So Jacob served seven years to get Rachel,*
> *but they seemed like only a few days to him*
> *because of his love for her.*
> *Genesis 29:20*

Our school class in 1944. I am sitting on the first row farthest to the right.

School

I don't remember starting school, even though I was eight years old at the time. They only enrolled new children every other year, which is why I had to wait until I was eight years old.

The school was in Karshult about four kilometers away. We walked to and from school every day, and Linnea complained that it was uphill and against the wind both ways! In the winter, if the roads were packed with snow or ice, we could use the kick sled. Sometimes we would have two or three feet of snow covered with a thick frozen crust that held to walk on, until suddenly a foot broke through and we found ourselves waist deep in snow. In the spring, summer and fall, when the ground was bare and not icy, we sometimes bicycled to school. We had a couple of bicycles, but not enough for everyone, so we had to double up.

One day we were on our way home and I had Birgitta on the back of my bike. She got her foot caught in the back wheel and it cut a chunk off of her heel.

It was a country school with only one classroom and one teacher. Our teacher taught all grades, but since enrollment was every other year, he would teach 1st, 3rd, and 5th grades one year, and the next he would teach 2nd, 4th and 6th grade. Terribly shy, I barely spoke to anyone in school. Even among my peers I was shy and I had very few friends. Alva, who lived about a mile from us, was my best friend.

Our teacher was such a wonderful, kind, Christian man. We started each school day by singing a hymn and saying a prayer. Then we had our Christian studies lesson, which was my favorite. I also enjoyed science and math.

Another class photo. I'm that tall girl
standing in the back row, farthest to the left.

I didn't consider myself to be very clever, and always felt that I was the dumbest student in the class. Then one day I caught my friend, Elsa, peering at my math paper to see what I was doing. I was shocked and a little bit proud to find that someone would actually think I was smarter than them and would try to get my answers!

I wasn't very interested in geography and I really hated history! That's funny, since I have since then enjoyed traveling around the world, and now find history to be extremely fascinating.

During recess and for P.E. we often played a game called "Brännboll" (Burn ball). It is similar to baseball except that we used a longer stick and a smaller ball. You don't have a pitcher. Instead, you toss the ball up yourself and then try to hit it as far as possible. If you get caught while running the bases, you were "burned." Two team captains would begin picking their teams. Of course, the boys were all picked first, but I was always one of the first girls to be picked. I guess I was pretty athletic.

We brought a lunch with us to school. Usually it was just two pieces of bread with a little butter. We ate outside if the weather was nice. If it was too cold, we ate in the cloakroom.

One day I had made myself a special lunch with a good sandwich and a thermos of hot chocolate. I was so happy when I hung my backpack on the handle of my kick sled and headed off to school, already anticipating my good lunch. My friend Alva met me when I reached the road and gave my sled a playful bump. The thermos broke and hot chocolate spilled out ruining my backpack and my special sandwich. My wonderful lunch was ruined and I was terribly disappointed.

We graduated after 6th grade. Ceremonies were held in the Lutheran church and everyone who graduated received a diploma. It was a big day for all of us.

Our little school in Karshult is now a summer house, but the school in Möcklehult has been renovated and is now the village hall and school museum, its walls covered with class photos from both schools. And yes, I am in many of them. I guess that makes me a museum piece!

Class reunion 2002

WWII

World War Two began in 1939. The adults followed the news on the radio and discussed the situation in front of us children. Everyone was afraid that Sweden would be the next country Germany invaded. In the evenings we had to cover our windows with heavy dark curtains so that no light could seep out. I remember being frightened when I saw a small airplane flying high above us in the sky. We didn't see many airplanes, and I was afraid it might drop a bomb on us. Although Sweden remained neutral throughout the conflict we had a lot of refugees from Finland and Germany, and 7,200 Jews were smuggled into Sweden via Denmark.

As if the war weren't enough, the winters of '39 and '40 were the coldest in modern history. Temperatures sank below –40 degrees Celsius, which is the same as –40 degrees Fahrenheit. We had beautiful cherry trees growing around the house. It got so cold that the bark on the trees exploded and all the trees died. How we missed those cherry trees!

The government ran out of fuel to heat the hospitals and essential buildings and there was very little firewood available to purchase. They passed a law commissioning every farmer who had forest to sell a certain amount of firewood to the government. They called it "commission wood." Although the government paid for the firewood, they didn't pay as much as the trees would be worth when they were later sold as lumber. My father and his friend, Otto, worked in the forest pulling up old roots and dead stubs and anything they could find that was burnable, so they wouldn't have to cut down his valuable trees.

As the war raged on certain food items became scarce. We had ration cards for bread, flour, sugar, coffee, butter and many other things. Since we lived on a farm and grew our own food we managed pretty well, but we did need to buy coffee, sugar and yeast. We roasted rye really dark and used it as a surrogate for coffee. My grandmother baked sourdough bread. She would save a piece of the dough to use the next time she baked. It saved on yeast and made really good bread.

We didn't suffer or starve, and didn't have to eat bark bread like my grandparents had done during the famine years of 1868-69. But going out to get water from the well or to bring in wood for the fire when it was −40 degrees outside was agonizing enough.

Lindö

We lived in southern Sweden, in the province of Småland, on a farm in Lindö. My mother called it the end of the world because it was so far from everything. It really was a beautiful place to grow up, a small farm with lots of forest and two lakes. Berries and mushrooms grew in the forest; fish were in the lake; we raised cows for milk and pigs for meat; and we grew grain and vegetables. My father, who had a passion for hunting, would bring home ducks, birds and deer.

Since we owned our own farm we were not considered poor, but my parents were very careful and thrifty. Our house was primitive. Downstairs we had a kitchen and a living room. Upstairs there was a small bedroom, a cold attic room and a room where we kept the loom. We had no running water and no electricity. During the long, dark winters we used candles or kerosene lamps for lighting. The only heat came from the wood burning stove in the kitchen and a smaller stove in the upstairs bedroom.

Hjälmseryd
Socken

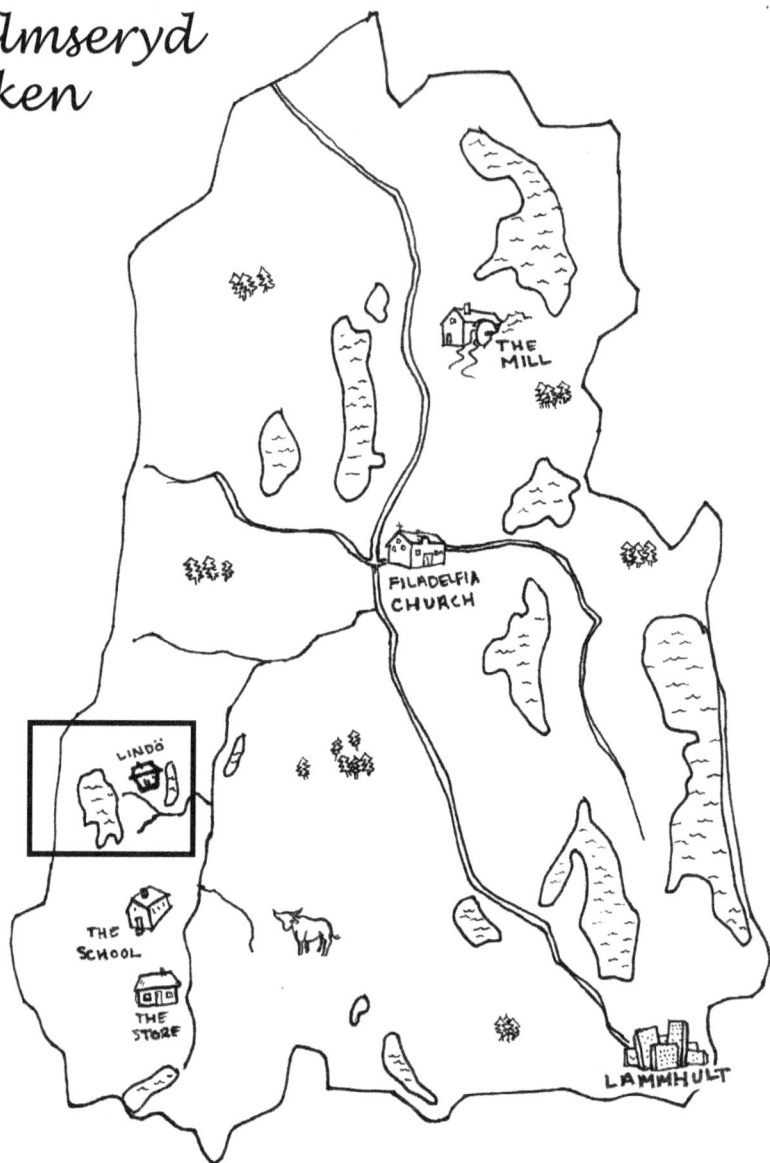

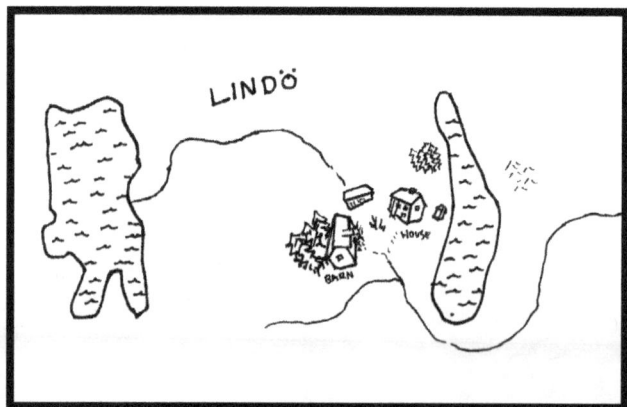

THE
MILL

FILADELFIA
CHURCH

LINDÖ

THE
SCHOOL

THE
STORE

LAMMHULT

LINDÖ

HOUSE

BARN

During the colder seasons we wore clogs, throwing them off on the porch before coming into the house. We weren't concerned about putting them in a row so there was often a huge pile of clogs that you had to climb over to enter the kitchen. When the weather began to get warm in the spring we cast off our shoes and ran barefoot over the gravel and fields, until the soles of our feet where thick like leather.

My father slept in the kitchen while the rest of us slept in one room upstairs. Before bedtime we would go up and light a small fire in the wood stove so that it would not be freezing cold when we came up later. Once in bed, I crawled under the many blankets and pulled them high over my head, warming the bed with my breath. I didn't freeze at night, as the covers kept me nice and warm, but in the morning it was biting cold. The first one up in the morning had to run down and light a fire in the kitchen stove so that it would be warm when everyone else came down.

In the fall we had "winter windows" that we put up inside the existing windows. A roll of cotton was place on the windowsill between the two windows to soak up the condensation. Then we taped around the inside windows so that the wind wouldn't blow through. In spring we would take the "winter windows" out and store them until fall came again.

In 1939, just before the war began, we had electricity installed in the house. It was a great day! All we had to do was turn a switch and the light would come on. Not only that, we also had a switch in the house which would turn on a light in the barn. We also bought an amazing box. When you turned the knob on the box, sound came out! It was a radio!

In 1945 they dug a trench from the well up to the house and installed a waterline. We had a pump in the kitchen and could get water from the well without going outside! There was no drainpipe to lead the water back out, instead we used a bucket to catch any drops. We had a large enamel bowl, half filled with water, where we washed our hands. We used the same water all day, and in the evening, when it was dirty, we threw it out the back door.

With electricity and running water, we felt really modernized. We still used the outhouse that was about 75 feet behind the house. There was no toilet paper; we used newspaper instead. We still didn't have a telephone. That wouldn't be installed until 1952.

There were two lakes on our farm. Göla was the closest, about 200 feet from the house. It was the source of most of our entertainment. It was a beautiful lake, but not for swimming. It had steep muddy edges, and a mud bottom, but that never bothered us. We found places where we could get in and out. There was an old stump about two feet from shore. We found a small crevice in the stump for our big toe, grabbed the top with our hands, and swung ourselves into the water. After years of use, that small crevice in the stump became a nice smooth hole. At the end of a hard day's work we would run down there and swim. I visited Lindö not too long ago. That stump is still there, and so is the hole we created with our big toes!

Swimming came naturally to us. I can't remember learning how to swim; it was just something we knew how to do. I decided one day to swim across Göla. It is six meters deep and 200 meters wide. It probably wasn't a smart thing to do, but I did it. One year I decided that I would swim every day until the lake froze over. It got colder and colder, I can remember the ice floating around me as I swam, but I kept at it. If you just put your mind to it you can do just about anything.

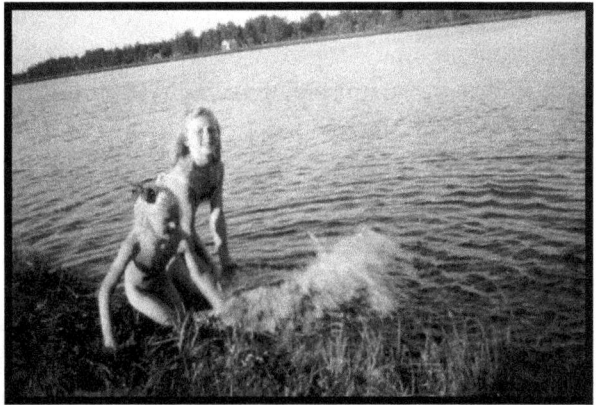

Birgitta and I playing in Göla.

The other lake was about a kilometer away through the forest. Ljungsjön was actually a nicer lake with a gravel bottom, but it was full of bloodsucking leeches so we didn't swim in it. Instead, we took the rowboat out and went fishing, usually rowing to the other side. Fishermen always think the fish bite better on the other side.

Solveig made a fishing pole by tying a string to a tree branch and attaching a hook to the other end. She made a bobbin out of a cork and a chicken feather and attached it to the line. Fishing on Ljungsjön by herself one day, she came home with 42 fish!

But fish are moody and they don't always bite. I was fishing on Göla one day and the fish were just not biting. Mother had told me to be home by six o'clock. I prayed and prayed that I would catch a fish, but I had decided that I would be obedient and come home on time.

Solveig fishing on Ljungsjön, 2007

Just as I was getting ready to pull in my line and leave, I caught it, a nice big perch! You can believe what you like, but I believe it was an answer to prayer.

I made a contraption out of chicken wire that would allow a fish to come in but not to get out. My father didn't say anything, but he was laughing. I think he approved of my ingenuity but didn't think I would be able to catch anything. I put it in Göla and went to check it every day. For a long time I didn't catch anything. Then one day I had a fish, 12 inches long, in my cage. I was so proud!

In the winter I would ice fish. As soon as the ice was strong enough to walk on I would go out and cut a hole in the ice with an axe. I tied a string to a stick that I laid across the ice, attached a dead herring to the other end, and dropped it in the hole. Every day I went out onto the lake to check my line, but there was never anything on it. In the spring my father told me it was time to bring in the ice fishing tools. I used the kick sled to go out on the ice, because it was safer. When I reached my hole and pulled on the line I could feel it pulling back. I had caught a big pike that was 30 inches long! That was a day I'll never forget.

When it comes to fishing, as with so many other things, you just have to keep on keeping on and never give up. I would stand for hours with my homemade fishing pole. Sometimes I wouldn't get a bite, but sometimes I pulled in a big 'un!

The Critters

Our farm was self-sustaining. In the barn, which was about 150 feet from the house, we had one horse, five cows, two or three pigs and about 25-30 chickens. Sometimes we had a sow and she would have seven to eight piglets. If we were lucky we were able to watch her give birth. That was fun. When the piglets were big enough to leave their mother we sold them to other farmers. Pigs are really nice and they are good housekeepers, using one corner of the pen as a toilet area and keeping the rest of it nice and clean. Cows and calves go wherever, whenever, even while they are being milked! They would start spouting off at any time, and we would have to jump out of the way. Twice a day we had to go out to the barn and muck out behind the cows. Then we had to feed the animals and do the milking.

Winters in Sweden are dark. The sun doesn't come up in the morning until 9:00 and sets early at 3:00 in the afternoon. Before the electricity was installed in the barn we carried a small kerosene lantern so we could see where we were going and what we were doing.

Snow would brighten things up a bit, but if it snowed during the night we would have to dig a path to the barn before we could start our chores.

Sometime in the fall the cows would begin, one by one, to go into heat. We took turns leading the cows to a farmer who had a bull. One day my father tied a rope around the neck of a cow and told me to take her to a farm in Lida about four kilometers away. It wasn't difficult, as the cow followed along easily enough, but I was embarrassed. I didn't think any other kids had to do a job like that, and I hoped that no one from school would see me. When I arrived at the farm where they had the bull, I tied the cow to the fence and went to the house to tell them that I was there with the cow. The farmer came straight away and brought the bull out. I watched the whole procedure, paid the farmer and then walked home with the cow.

In the spring the cows began calving. We kept the female calves that would one day become milk cows, but we slaughtered the males. First we let the calf drink from his mother until he was full, and then we butchered him. Cattle have four stomachs and, since the calf had just eaten, the first one was full of curdled milk. We poured the contents of the calf's stomach in a bowl and mixed it with salt and cumin. Then we rinsed the stomach with a little water, not too much because we didn't want to remove all the enzymes, poured the milk back into the stomach and hung the whole thing up to dry over the stove. Once dry, it would hold for a long time. We used the culture, or rennet, to make cheese and cheesecake.

When the weather got warm enough it was time to let the cows and calves out to pasture. After being locked up in the barn for the whole winter, the cows were excited to be released. The calves were careful at first at this new encounter, but when they realized that it was safe they jumped and frolicked in the fresh grass. If you have ever seen the calves released in spring, you will understand what God meant in this verse:

But for you who revere my name, the sun of righteousness will rise with healing in its wings. And you will go out and leap like calves released from the stall.
Malachi 4:2

Every evening at about five o'clock we had to go out and round up the cows and bring them home. They could wander off one or two kilometers in any direction and we had to find them. That is why they wore bells around their necks. As long as they were moving around and grazing you could hear the bells ringing and follow the sound. Sometimes the cows had already settled down in the grass to chew their cud and the bells were silent. Then we had to search all over the place to find them. When we did finally find them they knew it was time to come home and came willingly.

I learned how to milk the cows when I was just seven or eight years old. There was a barn cat that would come and sit next to me whenever I was milking. I would shoot milk straight into his mouth and he liked that a lot.

After we had milked the cows we carried the milk into the house where we had the cream separator. We poured the milk into the separator and turned the handle around and around. Cream came out one spout and skim milk came out the other. We were allowed to drink all the skim milk we wanted and fed the rest to the calves. We made butter out of the cream, churning it in the same kind of butter churn you can find in antique stores today. It was kind of fun pushing that handle up and down until the cream turned into butter. When we were done we drank the buttermilk that was left over! Yumm!

We stopped separating the milk ourselves when we began selling to the creamery. Saving enough for our own consumption, we poured the rest into a big jug that I hung on the side of my bicycle and took out to the road on my way to school. It was about a mile out to the road, and when I got there I had to lift the jug up on a table that was two or three feet high. There was a little step to climb on so that it would be easier.

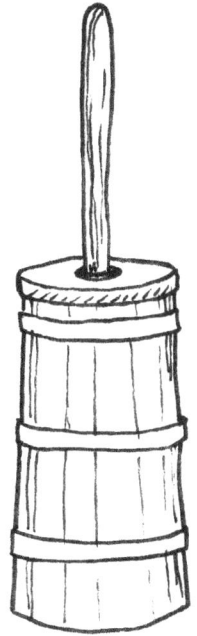

The creamery truck came by in the morning and picked up the jug. In the afternoon they brought the jug back full of skim milk that we fed to the calves. I would pick it up on my way home from school and bring it home on my bicycle.

Sometimes we saved the whole milk and made cheese. We used a piece of the rennet we had made from the contents of the calf's stomach, wrap it in cheesecloth and put it in a large pot of warmed milk. In about 20 minutes the milk had curdled. Pressing the curds together with our hands, we formed a lump that we then placed in a colander until the liquid had run off. Then we wrapped the cheeses in cheesecloth, pressing and forming them until we had squeezed out all the excess liquid, and put them on a shelf to age. They had to be turned every day so that they would age evenly. In about a month the cheese was matured and ready to eat. We baked bread with the liquid, or whey, that was left over from the cheese making.

Most people, if they didn't have a farm themselves, had family who did and could get cheese from them. Those who didn't had to buy their milk from the farmers. In our congregation there was one family who did not have their own milk. Once a year some of the farm wives would get together, bringing enough milk to make cheese to last the family an entire year. Laughter and gossip filled the air as the women worked at making cheese. These were women who usually worked in the fields. Their hands were dry and chapped, with deep cracks filled with dirt that could never be completely washed away, no matter how hard they scrubbed, but, when they had finished making cheese, their hands were just as white and clean as the cheese they were making.

In the fall we butchered one of the big pigs. The smaller children stayed inside the house while my father did the slaughtering, but I was older, so I got to watch. The pig screamed to high heaven all the way from the barn to the butchering area. It was as if he knew what was about to happen. Father stuck the knife right into the pig's neck and the blood began flowing into the bucket that Mother was holding. Stirring constantly so the blood wouldn't clump, she gradually added salt and flour. We used the blood for pancakes, pudding and sausage. Once all the blood had poured out, the pig had to be scrubbed in scalding water and shaved. Then father hung it up by its hind legs, cut open the stomach and pulled out the intestines. We used nearly every part of the pig. We cleaned the small and large intestines by turning them inside out and scraping them, using them later as sausage casings. We made liverwurst from the liver and headcheese from the head. The tongue made good sandwich meat. We even ate the ears and the feet. Pig's ears are crunchy and good and you can buy pig's feet in the store even today. I've heard that some people even used the bladder. They would take it out, drain it and rinse it. Then they put some dried peas inside, tied a string on both ends and hung it up to dry. It made a good ball with a nice rattling noise. We never did that, but it sounds like a good idea.

Some of the meat was ground to use for sausages, meatballs and other things. The rest was stored in a large barrel, weighed down with heavy rocks and covered in salt water to keep it fresh. We stored the pork barrel along with apples, potatoes, jams and jellies in the cellar underneath the house. When it was time to make dinner we would go down in the cellar, cut off a piece of salt pork and bring up a basket of potatoes. That was our most common meal.

Once, when my mother was hospitalized, we were in charge of the household. I went down before dinner to get a piece of pork. As I began frying it in the pan, I watched horrified as maggots began crawling out of the meat; they didn't like the heat. We had been sloppy about replacing the lid on the bucket and making sure the pork was underwater. Flies had gotten to the exposed meat and laid their eggs in it. I have never forgotten this experience and, every time I think about it, I can see the maggots coming out of the meat. I'm not especially squeamish, but this was just too much. I didn't know what to do with it; I just threw it out. That was one time that I really missed my mother.

One rooster and 20-30 hens occupied our chicken coop. In the spring we let the hens that were so inclined brood. It took 21 days until the eggs began to hatch, and we would have lots of little chicks. It was fun to watch them follow the mother hen wherever she went looking for food. The chicks would fight over the worms we dug up for them, pulling on each end in a tug-of-war. That was our summer entertainment. When they got tired they would crawl under their mother's wings. As the chicks grew, we could see which ones would be hens and which would be roosters. When they were big enough, we would go out, catch a young rooster or two, and wring their necks. Sometimes they would run around even after they lost their heads, and we would have to catch them again. Then they had to be cleaned and plucked. It was lots of work, but it made a good dinner.

We had two lakes on our farm, and they were both full of fish. Sometimes we would only catch small perch, but sometimes we caught a nice big pike. The females had eggs that were good fried, as good as any Russian caviar!

Sometimes we caught crawdads, but never enough to make a meal. They can survive a long time above water. My dad showed me how to hypnotize a crawdad. You just set it on its head and rub the tail. Pretty soon it will be asleep. If you bring me a crawdad, I'll show you how to hypnotize it.

My father also raised bees. In the summer when it was time to harvest the honey he would wear long sleeves and gloves and cover his head with a net. Bees get pretty angry when you mess with their hive. We had fun processing and canning the honey in the kitchen, safe from the bees.

Of course not all the critters on the farm were welcome or useful. We had a lot of flies. Strips of flypaper hung from the ceiling in the kitchen and the barn. Something on the paper attracted the flies and they would get stuck. Every available space on the strip was soon covered, but there were still plenty of flies to swat with the flyswatter. In the barn the cows carried "skamflugor," or louse flies. They walked sideways and backwards, staying primarily on the cows, but if you got one on you, they could crawl into your ears and cause a lot of problems. You couldn't kill them by swatting them; you had to wring their necks and break their heads off. Even then they would continue to run around headless for a while, just like the chickens.

There were also a lot of ticks. We just pulled them off, sometimes leaving the heads under our skin. We never realized they could be dangerous.

Our beds were infested with fleas. Every night we would check the seams in our quilts, killing the fleas by crushing them between our thumbnails. Hunting fleas was a never-ending task.

My mother took all this in stride, but she lived in perpetual fear that we would bring home head lice. If that happened, everyone's head would have to be checked, and those with lice had to be treated with a foul smelling solution. With all the little heads in our household, it was quite a job!

There are two kinds of snakes in Sweden, the Grass snake, which isn't poisonous, and the Viper, which is. Linnea was bitten by a viper when she was two years old. My parents were working about 500 yards from the house, and she was playing in the grass when the snake bit her on the hand. My father heard her scream and saw what had happened. He quickly tied a tourniquet around her arm and, leaving her with my mother, bicycled as fast as he could to Slättö, four kilometers away, where he could use the phone to call someone who had a car. They hurried to Lindö, to pick up Linnea, and then drove the 14 kilometers to Vrigstad, to the nearest doctor. Today they say that you shouldn't use a tourniquet, but I wonder if she would have survived without it.

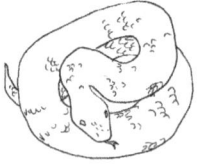

One day I was on walking on the other side of Ljungsjön at a place called Näset. Wild strawberries grew around a pile of rocks that had once been the foundation of a house, and I was picking them and eating them. Suddenly I spotted a snake sunning itself on a rock. I could see that it was a viper, and I knew I had to kill it. We didn't want vipers on our farm. Picking up a big stick, I snuck up and hit it on the head. It was dead, but from its belly came ten tiny baby snakes.

Now I really had a job! Using a stick, I carried the big snake over to a nearby anthill and deposited it among the ants. Then, one by one, I carried the baby snakes over to join their mother. The ants went crazy and before long they had devoured all of the snakes, large and small. I felt as if I had saved the world!

This story might be a little too much for some sensitive souls, but Orla Jens wanted me to tell everything just the way it was, so I will.

We had cats in the barn to keep the mice population under control. We didn't consider them pets; they served a specific purpose. In the summer some of them would get pregnant, as cats tend to do, and would have five or six kittens. We couldn't keep them, so we would follow the mother cat until we found where she had hidden her kittens, and then we would kill them. It was easiest to kill them early, before they opened their eyes.

One summer we were going to keep one kitten. I asked my mother if I could choose the kitten if I killed the others. Nobody really cared which kitten we kept, so she said that it would be o.k. I chose the kitten I thought was the prettiest. The others I grabbed by their hind legs, slammed their heads against a sharp rock, and threw them on the dung pile. It didn't bother me any more than killing flies, fleas or mice.

On a farm, animals are either food or workers. If they aren't either, or if you have too many, you kill them. We killed mice and fed them to the cats, we killed snakes and fed them to the ants. Flies, fleas and mosquitoes we killed and just let drop to the ground.

We slaughtered pigs and male calves, and chopped the heads off half-grown roosters, and they later appeared on our dinner table. Unlike many city people today, we knew where our food came from. We caught fish and ate them. I've never understood the practice of "catch and release," seems cruel to me. Sorry fishermen!

Everything that lives and moves will be food for you.
Genesis 9:3

A Farm Year

*I*n addition to caring for the animals we also had fields to prepare, sow and harvest. In the fall, after the harvest, father would plow the field and then let them rest over the winter.

Spring

As soon as the ground thawed in the spring it was time to begin preparing the fields for planting. We had a harrow with big iron springs that dug deep into the dirt. After that we would smooth out the field by going over it with a smaller harrow that had shorter tines going down about six or seven inches in the ground. I liked that one; it didn't get stuck as often as the big harrow. By the time I was nine or ten years old I was handling the horse, driving back and forth over the fields, preparing them for seeding.

After harrowing we spread the manure. Every spring we moved all the dung from behind the barn and spread it on the

54

fields. We did it all by hand, loading
it on a wagon with a pitch fork and
a shovel and then driving it out to the
field and spreading it out. It was a dirty
smelly job. Spreading manure is heavy work
so Father did most of it, but we had to help.
We also cleaned out the outhouse. Father said we
couldn't use human excrement in the vegetable and
potato fields, so we spread it out on the grain fields.

Now that the fields were prepped, it was time for
planting. This was my father's job. We grew mainly oats, wheat
and rye. Father sowed the fields by hand just like the farmers
in the bible. Seeds that fell on the large boulders in the field
had to be brushed off so that nothing was wasted. When the
field was seeded we used the harrow again to make sure that the
seeds were buried in the ground. The last step was to drive the
horse around the field one more time with a heavy compactor
made of wood and iron. Compacting the ground insured that
the seeds stayed put and also helped keep the moisture in the
ground.

When the fields were sown, it was time to plant potatoes and
vegetables. First, we had to sort through the potatoes to find the
healthy ones. By spring many of the potatoes were rotten or had
begun to grow. I remember sitting in the cellar sorting potatoes for
hours. Father spread out manure on the field, harnessed the horse
to the plow and began to dig a furrow. We followed behind with
buckets full of planting potatoes, placing them at intervals along
the furrow. While father drove the plow back, covering
the potatoes as he went, we filled our buckets so
we would be ready for the next furrow. On and
on it went. We had to have enough potatoes to
last for a whole year, so the potato field was very
large. We ate potatoes everyday, salted pork and
potatoes, and mother would make a white gravy
out of pork fat, flour and milk.

Our vegetable garden was not as big as the other fields, so all the work, the digging and planting, was done by hand. We grew lettuce, sweat peas, red beats, carrots and rutabagas. The carrots and rutabagas would last awhile in the cellar, but we ate the other vegetables fresh. Summer was a wonderful time, we had fresh vegetables, fruit, berries and, of course, rhubarb that came up every year. I would pick a stalk and rub a cube of sugar on the end. Yumm! That was good!

Summer

I remember the long summer days in Sweden where the sun sets just barely in time for it to begin to rise again. Summer nights are never really dark, the last gleams of dusk fading away just before midnight, while the first light of dawn seeps into the sky around two o'clock in the morning. The forests are alive with the twitter of birds; deer and moose are teaching their babies to forage for food; the fish are jumping in the lake.

Summer is a hectic time on a farm; there is always something to do. When we finished seeding the fields and planting the potatoes and the vegetable garden, it was time to cut the hay. Father would cut our large clover field. Then he would cut every little strip or corner of grass that could possibly be hay. In the bigger fields we hung the hay up on racks to dry. In the smaller areas we just raked it away from trees and shrubs so that it would dry in the sun. The trick was to get it dry and into the barn before it rained.

One Sunday after church we saw a thunderstorm brewing. The hay was dry and ready to be brought in, but we weren't supposed to work on Sunday. Father looked at the sky and said, "Never mind, let's get the hay in." He harnessed the horse to the big hay wagon and we all helped. Two kids stood in the wagon, stomping down the hay as it was piled on. There was a ramp, built out of rocks and then covered with dirt, leading up to the second floor of the barn. We drove the wagon up the ramp right into the hayloft. In the barn father unloaded the hay onto the floor and then two kids would move it over to the wall, stuffing it in to fill every possible space. Father spread salt over the hay to keep it fresh and then we would go out and get another load. We had to get the hay into the barn before it began to rain. It was hard work but we did it. The hayloft was full from floor to ceiling. When we were done our bodies itched from sweat, salt and dust. Jumping in the lake never felt so nice!

Although we were criticized for working on Sunday, Father didn't apologize for his actions. I guess he figured that God knew that we needed to get the hay inside.

"If any of you has a sheep
and it falls into a pit on the Sabbath,
will you not take hold of it and lift it out?
Matthew 12:11

Summer time was also the time to do laundry. Once a year we stripped the beds, all the sheets and pillowcases. Mother boiled the sheets in a huge pot to get them clean. Then we beat them with a wooden paddle, rinsed them in cold water and hung them on the line to dry. While the sheets were drying we would fill our mattresses with fresh straw so they would be nice and full when we put the sheets back on.

Although we only washed the sheets once a year, we washed our clothes whenever there was time during the summer. Again we used the big wash pot, scrubbing the clothes on a corrugated washboard. I'm sure you've seen those washboards in books or antiques stores; I have one on the wall in my laundry room just to remind me how easy it is to do laundry today. It was hard to do laundry in the winter. Of course we always had diapers that needed to be washed. Whenever possible we hung them outside on the line but, more often than not, they were hung in the kitchen.

Småland is called the "kingdom of rocks" and our fields were full of them. Whenever he had some time my father would go out and dig up the rocks. Sometimes, if it were an especially large rock, he would drill a hole, fill it with dynamite and blow it to pieces. Many times he would get us all out in the field to pick up the small rocks and the pieces that had been created by the dynamite.

As I said, there was no end to the work. One year my father had cut down some trees. He shaved the bark off in long strips while it was still in the forest. Linnea and I had to carry the bark strips from the forest up to the road where it could be picked up with a horse and wagon. What a terrible job! I remember it was midsummer's eve, and we carried load after load. We kept hoping that father would say, "That's enough for today, it's midsummer." But it was in the middle of the war; no one was celebrating, and we worked a full day.

Another job we hated was working with peat. Found in marshlands around the lakes, peat forms when layer after layer of vegetation dies and only partially decays. After many centuries the peat can be several feet deep. Father and his friend, Otto, dug out thick squares, creating a ditch that ran all the way to the lake. We had to carry the squares up and spread them out to dry. After a few days, when one side had dried, we'd turn the squares over to dry on the other side. When it had dried completely we stacked the blocks and stored them in a shed near the marshland. When we ran out of peat in the barn we would bring the horse and wagon down to the shed, fill it with dried peat, and bring it back to the barn. There, it had to be ground up and stored. We used peat in the barn, spreading it behind the cows to soak up the moisture and urine. It gave the manure a better consistency, making it easier to spread and it also helped to hold the moisture in the fields. Once, when I was spreading peat in the calf pen, a calf came too close and I poked him in the eye with the pitchfork. I felt so bad. The calf walked around with his head tilted up. I told Linnea what had happened and begged her not to tell anyone. No one ever mentioned it, and neither did I.

I remember one summer day our parents decided to take a day off. Mother packed a picnic with good sandwiches and some chocolate. She even bought a pack of cigarettes. We seldom had a day off so we were all excited. We walked to Hultet which was about three or four kilometers away on the other side of Ljungsjön. All that remained of the small house that had once stood there was the foundation and an overgrown garden. Father fetched water from the spring. It was as sweet and clear as could be. (O.K. it had a few mosquito larvae floating in it, but we strained them through our teeth.) I remember Father said that you couldn't find a better drink. It was a wonderful, fun day. We enjoyed seeing our parents splurge a little and enjoy a day off. The only down side was that father insisted on bringing the cows with us so that they could graze on the other side of the lake. Linnea and I had the job of watching them and rounding them up when it was time to go home.

. Lingonberries and blueberries grew wild in the forest; raspberry brambles bordered the fields and cloudberries grew on the marshlands around the lake. Our household needed a lot of berries and we picked as much as we could. My mother made "saft" from the blueberries. Cooking the berries with and equal amount of sugar and a little water, she made a concentrate that, mixed with water, made a punch free from artificial ingredients or preservatives. The bottles were dipped in wax to seal the cork and then stored in the cellar.

We ate lingonberries everyday, on our oatmeal, with dinner and sometimes as desert with milk. We needed enough to last the whole year. Mother made a jelly that is a lot like the cranberry sauce we eat at Thanksgiving. She cooked the lingonberries with sugar and then stored them in a big barrel in the cellar.

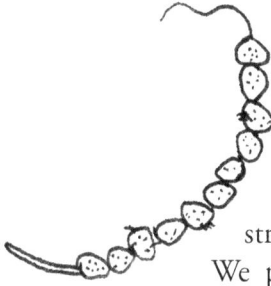

Tiny wild strawberries grew on the sunny slopes by the road and around the stone walls. They are sweet, and taste slightly different than regular strawberries. We picked them, threaded them on a long strand of grass, and gave them to our mother.

We picked raspberries and ate them fresh, but you had to check them for worms. To this day I have trouble eating raspberries.

Nettles grew all over the place. In the spring when the first leaves appeared, we would take a bowl and a pair of scissors and go out and pick them. Careful not to burn our fingers on the leaves, we cut them and let them fall into the bowl. Then mother would make soup. Nettle soup is really good and nutritious, similar to spinach soup, and they don't burn when they have been cooked!

By August the wheat, oats and rye had grown tall and was ready to harvest. Again father went first with the scythe and cut it down one row at a time. We followed after, picking up enough to make a sheave and then tying it with straw. It was hard work. Rye was the worst. It was coarse and it scratched your arms. I wore long sleeves or had a pair of old socks pulled over my arms to protect them, but when the day was over they would be red and scratched anyway.

One year we were harvesting rye on August 31st. With every row I hoped Father would say we could quit because it was my birthday. But he didn't, and we worked the whole day.

When we finished cutting and tying the sheaves, we bundled four together so they would stand up, and left them to dry in the field. Once they were dry they were loaded on the wagon and driven into the barn. Father stood in the wagon and threw the sheaves out on the floor where two of us kids were waiting to carry them to the back. They had to be laid out in rows so that they fit neatly, and it would be easy to take them down again when it was time to do the threshing in the fall.

Fall

Potatoes were harvested in the fall. We did this by hand with a hoe. We worked in pairs, each taking a row, and had two big baskets between us. We sorted the potatoes as we dug them up, the good ones going into one basket, and the bad ones, including those we happened to cut with the hoe, went into the other. There could be no bad potatoes mixed in with the good ones. We fed the bad potatoes to the pigs. If there was a large boulder in my row, I called them my "stone helper," because I could sit down and rest for a moment while my partner worked past me in her row. Picking potatoes was kind of fun. The baskets had a handle on each side. When one of them was full we each grabbed a handle and carried the basket to the wagon and emptied it. When the wagon was full, we had the horse pull it up to the house, where we filled the baskets again and carried the potatoes down to the big box in the cellar.

Some years, we had a field of sugar beets. Harvesting them was a lot of work because we piled them up outside and covered them with straw and dirt to keep them from freezing. In the spring we dug them up to feed the cows.

When the potatoes, carrots and rutabagas were stored in the cellar along with the barrel of lingonberry jelly, bottles of saft, and the barrel of salt pork, and father had plowed all the fields leaving them to rest over the winter, we began the threshing. The sheaves of wheat, oats and rye were brought down from the loft so that the kernels could be separated from the straw. This couldn't be done during the stressful harvest season, since there wasn't time, but it had to be done before the mice came in and ate all of it.

Before electricity was installed we had to do the threshing by hand. We spread the sheaves out on a wood floor and then beat them with a flail, two wooden sticks connected end to end by an iron loop. Grabbing one end of the flail we would swing the other end down hard on the sheaves until all the kernels had fallen off. When we were finished the floor would be full of kernels, straw, and small pieces of seed head, called chaff. We collected the straw with a rake and stored it away until later. Then we separated the kernels from the chaff by sweeping them up and throwing them across the room. The chaff, which was lighter, fell quickly to the ground, while the kernels landed by the opposite wall.

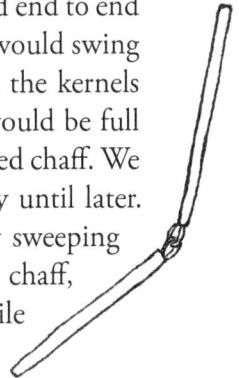

As soon as the electricity was installed, my father went out and bought a threshing machine. This made threshing so much faster and easier.

Father stood at one end of the machine feeding it with sheaves. A couple of us stood at the other end, collecting the straw that came out, and moving it away from the machine and up into the loft. Nice, clean kernels of grain spewed out of the side of the machine, ready to put into the sacks.

When the threshing was done, the sacks of grain had to be taken to the mill, 11 kilometers away, on the other side of Hjälmseryd. I was about twelve years old when my father said, "May-Britt can take the horse and drive it to the mill." He loaded the wagon with sacks of oats, wheat and rye. I wasn't quite sure how to get there but Father said, "The horse knows the way." And he did.

Grinding the grain into flour took all day, so I had to wait. I ate the lunch I had with me, and waited some more. When the sacks of flour were loaded up on the wagon we started towards home. Our big workhorse became skittish when a car rushed past, but I was able to control him. Luckily traffic was light back then. I was so proud when I drove up to the farm with the wagon full of bags of flour. Mission accomplished.

The straw that had been stored up in the loft during threshing now had to come down again. We had a machine with a very large, very sharp blade that cut it up into small pieces we called "hackelse." There were a lot of things we worked with on the farm that were really very dangerous. It's amazing there were not more accidents. The "hackelse" was mixed with molasses and fed to the animals. They loved it, and ate it like candy.

When you see a Swedish farm with the red buildings nestled in the clearing, cows grazing in the field, wheat growing tall and golden, a lake glistening off to the side and the smell of forest filling the warm summer air, it seems so idyllic, so peaceful.

But I will never forget the endless days spent following my father across the fields planting potatoes, or the harvest when our arms were scratched red from the course rye. I can still feel the sweat and salt on my skin and the extreme exhaustion we felt after bringing in the hay. When the day was over we would all run down to the lake and swim away the heat and dust, and the fatigue that weighed our limbs down seemed to run off with the dirt leaving us, refreshed and invigorated.

Winter

Winter days are short, dark and cold. The sun climbs half way up in the sky, only to change its mind and go down again in mid-afternoon. Snow free winters can be as dark as the inside of your hat, but when the snow falls, it brightens even the darkest night.

Occasionally we would hear a loud bang coming from the electrical wires. We thought a grouse, a large forest bird with a very wide wingspan, might have flown into the wires and been electrocuted. We searched the ground the next day, following the wires, but we never found one. It would have made a good dinner.

I remember coming home late one winter night around eleven o'clock. Fiery flames of red and green danced across the sky. It looked like a forest fire, but there was no smoke. I had never seen the Northern Lights before and didn't know what it was. It was breathtaking. What a fascinating world we live in! God's creation is so amazing.

Wintertime was a time to catch up on all the jobs that we didn't have time to do the rest of the year. Father repaired tools and farm equipment. He went hunting, and worked a lot in the forest, cutting down trees that he sold for lumber or brought home to be chopped for firewood.

We didn't have any sheep but we bought wool from a neighbor. When the weather began to get warm in late spring, early summer, they would give the sheep a good scrubbing and then shear them. It was easier to wash the wool while it was still on the sheep than to wait and wash it after the shearing was done.

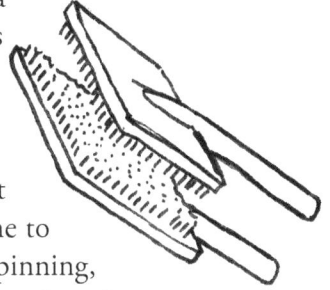

We brought the wool home and stored it away until winter when there would be time to spin it into yarn. Preparing the wool for spinning, we carded the wool with two flat, wire brushes that combed the knots out and rolled the wool into fluffy lengths.

I remember my mother at the spinning wheel. She made it look so easy. I tried, but I was never very good at it, I could never get the yarn even. We learned to knit socks and mittens and to darn them when they wore out. It's amazing the things we had time to do back then. Today, despite all our timesaving devices, time seems to be our most precious commodity.

Nothing whatsoever was ever wasted. I don't think we even owned a trash can. Leftover food was given to the pigs, old newspapers were used as toilet paper, and worn out clothing was cut into strips and used to make rugs. Mother had a loom in the room upstairs on which she wove beautiful rag rugs. Our job was to cut the rags into long strips and roll them into balls. They were sorted by color and she would weave nice patterns in the rugs.

Holidays

Christmas

Christmas was the highlight of the year, something we waited for and anticipated all year. We were out of school for three weeks and, although we still had the barn and the animals to care for, there were fewer chores. Preparations began early so that we would have everything ready in time and there were lots of parties.

We slaughtered the pig in November so the cellar was full of sausages, meatballs, blood pudding, headcheese, and a barrel of salt pork. We bought a big stack of lutfisk to eat during December. Lutfisk is North Atlantic Cod that has been cleaned and then stretched out on a frame or rock to dry in the sun and the wind until it is as hard as a board. Dried, like this, it will last for years and still retain most of its nutrients. They say that the longer you store it the tastier it gets, but you don't eat it dry. It took three weeks to prepare the "Lutfisk." First we soaked it in water for a week, replacing the water daily, until it began to soften. Taking ashes from the stove, we made a lye solution, or "lut." The stove had to be cleaned out periodically, so this was a good time to do it. We soaked the fish in the "lut" for another week, being careful so it wouldn't get too soft. After that it had to be soaked in water, again changing the water daily, for another week. Finally it was ready to cook. Lutfisk is served boiled, with potatoes and white gravy. We thought it was a nice break from the salt pork we otherwise ate. I can't understand why so many Americans don't like Lutfisk. Perhaps if they knew how much work went into it they would appreciate it more. Of course, today you can buy it ready to cook, and you don't have to go through the effort of preparing it.

Mother started baking in mid-December, making lots of different kinds of cookies. Tradition dictated that you had to have a least seven kinds of cookies when you had company for coffee. She made Finnish sticks, jam cookies, dreams, almond cookies, farmers cookies, and more. Later on she would bake cinnamon rolls and coffee bread.

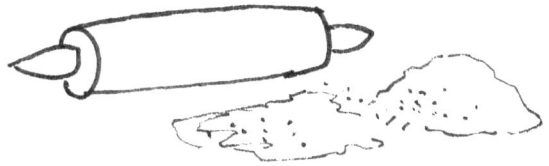

Baking in a wood-burning oven took some skill to maintain just the right temperature, but my mother knew just how to control it. My father would taste her cookies and say, "She really knows how to bake!"

Sometime before Christmas she made Pepparkakor, or ginger cookies. She would make enough dough so that we each could have a piece, and we were allowed to make cookies in any shape or form we wanted. We had a lot of fun baking pepparkakor, and created lots of memories. I kept this tradition with my own children, and have passed it on to my grandchildren.

The first big day of the Christmas Season is the 13th of December, St. Lucia Day. Saint Lucia was martyred for her faith in Italy during the forth century. Not wanting to marry a pagan, she consecrated herself to God and donated her dowry to the poor. Her would-be husband denounced her as a Christian and she was sentenced to death. When the soldiers arrived to drag her to the stake to be burned she was reportedly filled with the Holy Spirit and became too heavy to be moved. Instead, the soldiers gouged out her eyes and stabbed her to death. Her name means, "the way of light," and she is the patron saint of the blind. For some reason she is more celebrated in Sweden than she is in Italy. Her day is a celebration of light during the darkest day of the year.

Traditionally the oldest daughter gets up early to bring coffee and cookies to her parents who are still in bed. She is dressed in a long white dress with candles in her hair and she sings the Lucia song as she walks slowly through the house to her parent's bedroom.

Lucia is a big event in Sweden today. Nearly every small town or village elects a young girl to be Lucia. Girls between the ages of 16 and 19 are nominated, their pictures appearing in the newspaper, and the community is asked to vote. The winner is crowned with a crown of candles, and the other girls are her maidens. Dressed in white with a red sash, they'll make appearances during the week that follows Lucia Day, singing Christmas Carols, at restaurants, businesses, schools and hospitals. In Stockholm the Lucia pageant is broadcast nation wide. One Christmas, when I was working in a factory, I was elected to be the company Lucia.

I have incorporated Lucia into our Christmas celebrations. My grandchildren love to dress up as Lucia. They wear the white dress with a red sash, and a crown of battery-driven candles as they dance around the house and serve pepparkakor.

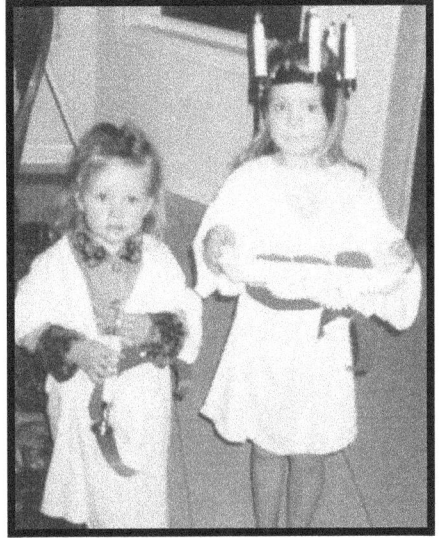

We also made Knäck, a homemade candy common at Christmas time. It is fairly easy to make with only five ingredients. The hardest part is cooking it long enough to get the right consistency, not too hard and not too soft. Today, my son makes the Knäck on Christmas Eve, a tradition that I hope he will pass onto his children.

Knäck

1 cup sugar
1 cup white Karo syrup
1 cup heavy cream
1/2 cup almonds - blanched and chopped

Put the three first ingredients in a heavy bottom pot. Let boil over medium heat for 20-45 minutes until it passes the ball test. Ball test: Drop a small amount of the knäck mixture in a glass of cold water. If you can roll the drop into a ball then the knäck is done!
Stir in the almonds and then spoon into small paper cups or pour out on a cookie sheet. Be careful, it's hot!
Let cool and cut into pieces.

My mother gave us all a bath the day before Christmas Eve, whether we needed it or not. Of course we needed it; we didn't take many baths. We all used the same water, soap and towel to get clean, and then we put on clean underwear. What a day! This was the best we could do as far as cleanliness, but it didn't bother us since we'd never had anything else. We never had a toothbrush either, nor would we have known what to do with one. But I'll tell you, I sure am glad I have one today, and I never take my morning shower for granted!

It wasn't easy to do a thorough cleaning in a house with four or five kids, with everyone having to work in the barn, but Mother had done what she could to make the house clean for Christmas. The kitchen had been cleaned after all the baking, the stove cleaned out when we did the Lutfisk. Now, when everyone was bathed and clean, she used the bath water to scrub the floors.

Christmas Eve morning we awoke excited, but the chores had to be done in the barn even though it was Christmas. Even the animals had a part of Christmas. In the barn, the horse got extra oats and the cows and pigs were also given something extra. Outside, we hung a sheave of oats in the tree in front of the kitchen window for the birds. Lots of birds would come and eat; many of them were as pretty and colorful as any Christmas tree ornament you hang on the tree.

When the chores were done in the barn, we went out and cut down the tree we had picked out months earlier. We were very particular about our tree and searched the forest all summer and fall until we found the perfect one. Bringing it into the kitchen, we attached a simple wooden foot, and decorated it with homemade ornaments and live candles.

One year I had made a bunch of Christmas decorations out of paper. I presented them to my mom but, being stressed and overworked, she blurted out, "I don't want all that junk." Heartbroken, I ran up the stairs and started to cry. She found me sitting on the steps, crying. "I'm so sorry. I made a mistake. Of course I want your decorations," she said with her arms around me. It felt so good to be comforted by my mother. We went downstairs and decorated the tree with all my junk. Today, I am careful to show my enthusiasm when my grandchildren bring me their creations.

We placed a bouquet of oats, decorated with foil and colorful candy wrappers, in the middle of our Christmas table. I remember thinking that it was quite pretty. At about eleven o'clock, it was time for coffee. We were allowed to take one of each of the seven kinds of cookies and a roll.

Father made the "Dopp i grytan," or "Dip in the pot," which was our special Christmas food. He made broth with some bones, and then added beef and pork, onions and spices. He removed the bones and the meat when everything was cooked and made gravy out of the broth, using a little flour and cream. We dipped a piece of bread in the gravy pot, which is why it is called, "Dip in the pot," and ate it together with the meat and potatoes.

After dinner, Mother would give us each a present. There was never much money for gifts, but she liked to buy something for each of us. She would buy the presents early and hide them and we would search high and low, trying to find our gifts before Christmas.

One year we each received a small chocolate pig. I left mine sitting on the tile stove we had in the living room. We didn't usually have a fire in there so both the oven and the room stayed cool.

Linnea snuck in there and dug the belly out of my pig. I was about to complain to my mother, but before I could do that I realized that they had lit a fire in the tile oven, and all that was left of my pig was a puddle of chocolate.

We ended the day with rice porridge. Mother put one almond in the bowl, blanched so that it was the same color as the porridge. Something good would happen to the person who got the almond, and we were all held in suspense until some called out, "I got it!"

One winter, during the war, Father was called into military service. Linnea and I were so happy, thinking that Christmas would be so much more fun when he wasn't there. He was so strict; when he wasn't around we were pretty wild. It must have been difficult for my mother, but she would never tell him.

On Christmas Day, at 6 o'clock in the morning, there was always a service in the church. My parents could never go because there was always a small baby at home, but Linnea and I would walk the seven kilometers to our grandparent's house on Christmas Eve, spending the night so that we could be in church at six o'clock in the morning. People came from all over, some walking, some by kick sled and others came by horse and sleigh. I remember the sound of the sleigh bells coming across the snow-covered hills.

If our whole family went somewhere during the winter, my father would hitch up the horse to the sleigh and we, too, would sail across the snowy landscape. It was so peaceful. All we could hear was the sound of the runners against the snow, and the ringing of the horse's bell. I still have the bell our horse once wore; it sits on my mantle and is one of the treasures I have from my childhood.

Christmas Day at home was fairly quiet. I remember that we sometimes had oranges, though certainly not during the war, that we would slice up and share. To this day the smell of oranges reminds me of Christmas.

The parties began on the second day of Christmas, the 26th of December. We would have a coffee and invite our neighbors from Kroxhylte and Skärshult. Then we would be invited to their houses the following days. This is when all the cookies came out. Every respectable housewife had to serve at least seven different kinds of cookies, plus coffee cake. I remember they sometimes made fun of one of the women because, although she baked seven kinds of cookies, she baked them all from the same dough and that was not acceptable. It was all in fun, though, and I don't think anyone was offended.

We never celebrated the New Year, or did anything special on New Year's Eve. When we were older Linnea and I walked to Hjälmseryd to attend the mid-night service at the Pentecostal church.

Christmas lasted until the 13th of January when it was time to dance it out of the house. We invited my friends, Alva and Elsie, to come over and help us. The tree was decorated with homemade ornaments and baskets, and inside each ornament or basket was a piece of candy. Undressing the tree, we tore open the ornaments and gobbled down the candy, knowing that we would make new ornaments next Christmas. Then we danced around the Christmas tree. Later, taking it with us outside, we dragged it around in the snow giving the younger children a ride. Finally, when we had tired of our game, the tree, now naked and bare, was thrown on the woodpile.

When my sister, Solveig, and I lived in California with our families we would celebrate a Swedish Christmas together. We called it "Lilla Jul." We would have ham and "Dip in the pot," and rice porridge with one almond, and we would dance around the Christmas tree. Later, when our children were grown and we moved to Colorado, we began to celebrate our Swedish traditions on Christmas Eve together with friends and family. We eat our traditional Christmas dinner complete with rice porridge and an almond. Our grandchildren dress up as Lucia with candles in their hair. Our son cooks the knäck. We dance around the tree and get a visit from Santa Claus. Sometimes we exchange one gift, saving the others for our "American Christmas" on Christmas morning. As I grew older the strain of holding this annual party became too much, and my son, Orla Jens, and his wife, Darla, have taken over the burden. I am so pleased that they are willing, interested and enthusiastic about carrying on these traditions that have been so dear to me.

Easter

Easter was another highlight of the year, we had two weeks vacation from school and were allowed to eat all the eggs we wanted. We cut branches from the birch trees, decorated them with colored feathers and put them in water. They would begin to sprout leaves and we knew that spring would soon be here.

Easter, in Sweden, is an interesting mixture of paganism and Christianity. I suppose it is that way with many holidays, but it seems more prevalent at Easter. On the one hand Easter meant bunnies, chicks and eggs, and, believe it or not, witches. Children dress up as witches and go door to door passing out homemade Easter cards, hoping to get a piece of candy or a coin in return. It may seem strange to see witches at Easter, but people once believed that evil spirits were especially active around Easter and that the witches all flew away to a meeting at an obscure place called "Blue Hill." People built bonfires to keep the witches and evil spirits away. Even now, Easter Eve is celebrated with a bonfire and firecrackers.

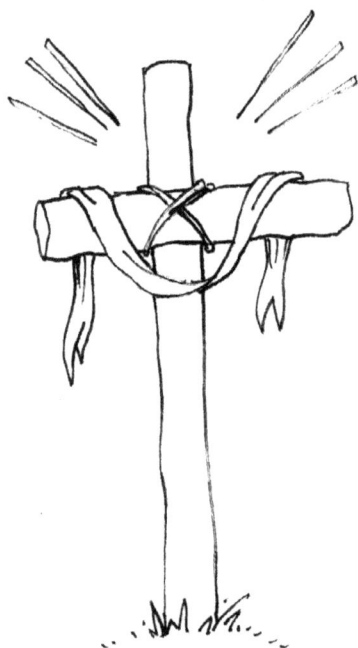

On the other hand many aspects of the religious holiday were observed. Good Friday is called Long Friday in Sweden, probably because it was a day that seemed to never end. All stores, theaters, restaurants, etc were closed, and all sorts of entertainment were forbidden. In really strict homes you were not allowed to do anything that was not absolutely necessary.

In our home, before my parents became Christians, we hardly noticed that it was Long Friday. Holiday or not, the animals had to be cared for, and when the chores were done we played outside or went fishing, and we were always allowed to read whatever we wanted. After we all became Christians we observed a more spiritual Easter by going to church. But I still remember Easter as the one time of the year that we could eat as many eggs as we wanted.

Mother's Day

Mother's Day, always the last Sunday in May, was the third biggest day of the year in our family. My mother baked two cakes and we all dressed in our Sunday finest. Father harnessed the horse to the spring wagon and we drove to my grandparent's house in Klerebo.

We had one gate that had to be opened as we drove along the road from Lindö. One of the kids would jump off the wagon and run and open the gate so that Father could drive the wagon through. Then they would close the gate and run

to catch up with us and jump back on the wagon. Some places in Sweden had many such gates and the children would wait around for a wagon to come by so that they could open the gate. If they were lucky the people in the wagon would throw them a coin. In the famous painting, Grindslanten, several kids are fighting over a coin the farmer has just thrown on the road. One little girl has spilled her basket of berries and is crying. We, of course, didn't get paid for opening the gate for our father, so we didn't have to fight over the coin.

When we came to Klerebo, where my mother's parents lived, we would have coffee and one of the cakes that my mother had baked. After visiting a little we would climb back in the wagon and drive to Ryd, where my father's parents lived. There, we would have dinner followed by many cakes and cheesecake. We had about 20 cousins on my father's side and the house would be packed. It was always fun to go there and play with everyone.

Midsummer

Although we don't have a midnight sun in Småland, where I grew up, in mid June the sun does not set until about 11 o'clock at night. It sets very slowly, giving us a long period of dusk, never quite reaching total darkness before it rises again sometime around 2 o'clock in the morning. Having survived the long, dark winter, Swedes celebrate the return of the sun by staying up all night on the eve of the summer solstice. Girls weave crowns of flowers to wear in their hair. (See my picture on the cover) A tall midsummer pole, dressed in birch branches and flowers, is raised and then they dance ring dances around the pole. We were told that if we picked seven different wildflowers and placed them under our pillow on midsummer's eve, we would dream of our future husband. I tried it, but I never dreamt of Orla. We never celebrated midsummer when I was growing up. It was in the middle of the war and we lived on a farm where summer time is the busiest time of the year. It wasn't until I was older that I attended some of the festivities.

Birthdays

We never celebrated birthdays although I occasionally got a gift from Linnea. Anna, the lady who lived deep in the forest, gave me a box of silver spoons when I turned 15. I have kept that box all these years and never used them. Today, after writing this down I polished them and found that they were beautiful. I guess I'll use them! Anna would never have imagined that her spoons would some day be used at a party in America.

My husband and children have more than made up for all the birthday celebrations I missed growing up. They have never missed a birthday. On my 40th birthday LaVonne and Orla Jens made a huge strawberry shake. Influenced by Farrell's Ice Cream Parlour, they began adding small toys to decorate the top. Carried away by their enthusiasm they continued to empty their toy box, adding cars, tops and even a tennis ball, until the whole thing was completely inedible! But I loved it.

My favorite birthday ended up being the one I dreaded the most. Turning 60 seemed to me to be the gateway to old age. I just wanted to forget the whole thing. I thought about escaping by flying to Sweden to surprise our daughter, but Orla was, for some reason, adamantly against me going. Instead we flew to Colorado Springs and Orla organized a party for me at a restaurant. Many of our friends were there and we all had a lovely time, but I was still a little depressed. Coming home to California on August 31st, my birthday, I was so tired. I told Orla I was just going straight to bed. I walked in the door and there was LaVonne standing in the family room with Jens and Darla singing "Happy Birthday." It floored me. She had come with her two small sons to stay with us for two months. Orla, of course, knew all about it, and together they had planned this incredible birthday surprise.

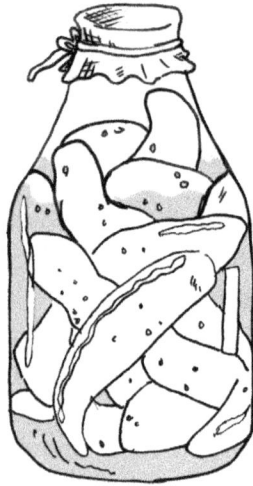

Entrepreneurship

I wasn't very old the first time I made money. My grandmother needed new bloodsucking leeches for her swollen legs. I went down to the lake and collected a jar full and bicycled nine kilometers up to her house in Ryd. I did it as a favor to her, not expecting to get paid, but she gave me three crowns. I felt like I had made a million dollars. That was the beginning of my entrepreneurship, and I have never stopped finding ways to make money.

Every summer we would pick berries in the forest. We needed a lot of berries for our household, but when we had picked enough to last us through the year we could pick and sell berries to the store. I made more money than anyone else picking lingon. I never gave up; I picked and picked until there were no more berries to pick. We even took the boat across Ljungsjön and picked berries on the other side of the lake.

Then I learned the benefits of wholesale. We used to pick two kinds of mushrooms that grew in the forests around our farm. Birgitta and Solveig had been out picking all day and

came home with a basket full of mushrooms. I offered to pay them ten cents for their mushrooms. They agreed. I bicycled the seven kilometers to Hjälmseryd and sold the mushrooms to the store owner, making a tidy little profit. My sisters are still a little miffed about that one.

In the winter I went from farm to farm, selling Christmas cards and Christmas magazines. Our neighbors were pretty spread out. By the time I came to Skärshult, walking up and down the long driveways to each house, I had walked about six kilometers. If there was snow, I could use my kick sled, which sure beat walking.

I also ordered frozen herring that came in a long narrow box. Dividing the fish into half-kilo portions, I packaged them in brown paper bags and then hit the road again. This was a great business. Nearly everyone bought my fish; it was a nice break from the salt pork they otherwise ate every day.

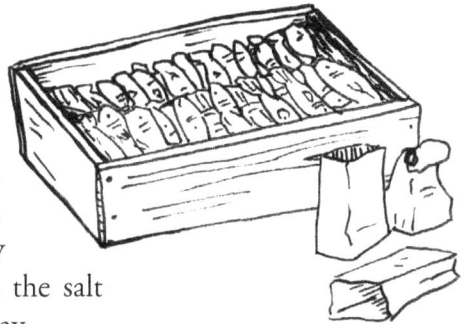

One day, when we were working in the field near the house, Father said that I could have the tree that grew on the edge of the field. It was a nice big pine tree. My first thought was that I could make some money. When the day's work was done I went and got an axe and a saw and cut the tree down. I had seen the men cut down trees many times so I knew how to make it fall in the right direction. Once I had it on the ground I cut off all the branches. Now I needed the horse to pull it out to the road where the lumber truck could pick it up. I asked my father if I could borrow the horse. I'm not sure that this is what he had in mind when he said that I could have that tree, but he wouldn't go back on his word. He helped me drag my tree out to the road. It was a big tree, almost a full truckload. Father said that when the lumber truck came, I could let them add some of his logs so that they would have a full load, and then I would still get the money for the whole load. I waited by the road for the truck to come and told the men what my father had said. Then I asked them to make sure they loaded the truck really full. The bigger the load, the more money I would make. I told them to take a big load, bigger than normal. They were very accommodating. How could they argue with a little girl who wanted to make some extra money? They loaded the truck so full that they couldn't make it up the steep hill in Skärshult and had to unload some of the logs and make two trips. But that wasn't my problem. I still got paid.

Firewood was a necessity. In early spring father would cut and chop enough firewood to last us a whole year. The pieces had to be small enough to fit into the stove that was used to cook our meals and to heat the house. He piled the wood outside the barn where it would dry over the summer. One day in the fall, he told me that if I carried all that wood into the woodshed, he would pay me three crowns. What a deal! Piling a load of wood on my arm, I ran up a plank and dropped them at the back end of the woodshed. I carried and carried, and carried some more. I don't know how long it took me, but I finally finished and got paid.

Despite my well developed work ethic I was not averse to cheating if the opportunity presented itself. One day I flattened a handful of pennies until they were the size of nickels. I couldn't use them in the store, of course, but I could fool the vending machine into dispensing candy.

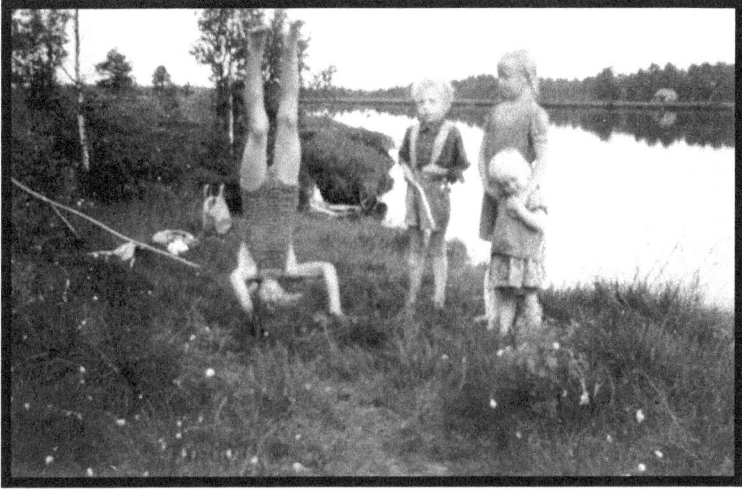

Things We'd Do For Fun

I walked a lot, just aimlessly wandering around the lake, through the forest and across the meadows. I remember one day I was crossing a bog when I saw a moose in front of me. It was a huge moose, with the biggest crown of antlers I had ever seen. He just stood there staring at me. Moose can be dangerous, especially large bulls, so I was looking around for a tree to climb. After a while, he turned around a walked away. Relieved I continued on my walk, no longer afraid.

Playthings

We didn't have many toys but I was good at making things. I made my own doll out of white material. I formed a body with two arms, two legs and a head. Then I asked my mother to sew the face. She did a really nice job sewing the eyes, nose and mouth with black yarn.

I was so proud of my doll. I made clothes for her, and a bed out of an old box. Later, I made another doll for Birgitta.

I took a hammer and a saw, got some planks and some nails, and built a playhouse behind the barn. It turned out really nice. Father chuckled at my ambitious project, but he didn't say anything. I don't know what he thought, but I think he was proud of me. Years later, when I had small children of my own, I wanted them to have a playhouse. I thought, "I've built one of those before, I can do it again." I found lumber, windows and a door at the junk yard, and started building one in the corner of our backyard. It was a lot of work, a lot more work than I remembered it being when I was a kid!

Winter fun

We used kick sleds in the winter as a means of transportation, but they were also a lot of fun. A kick sled looks like a kitchen chair on skis. You stand behind the chair with one foot on a runner and kick with the other. When you get up enough speed you can stand on both runners and just ride. Two people could stand on the back, one on either runner, with a passenger sitting on the chair. One Christmas Eve, Linnea and I took Birgitta with us to our grandparent's house. Halfway there we ran the kick sled into the ditch and Birgitta went flying.

As soon as Göla froze over we would be out on the lake with our kick sled. Solveig went out one day with the kick sled and an umbrella. There was a nice breeze and she picked up quite a bit of speed! But when she reached the other the end of the lake she had to come back by her own power and that wasn't quite as easy.

When I knew that we were going to have a cold night, I would cut a hole in the ice with an axe, put down a heavy 4x4 post and let it freeze solid overnight. Then I took a wooden pole, about ten feet in length, drilled a hole through it about 18 inches from one end, and put it down over a spike that was sticking out of the top of the post. On the other end of the pole I attached a toboggan or a kick sled. This was called a "Svängåka," or "Turnaround." Two or three people could sit on the toboggan while another person pushed the handle around and around.

In the winter, when it got really cold at night, we would pump water from the well and pour it over the ramp leading up to the second floor of the barn. When it had frozen we poured more water over it. Soon we had a thick sheet of ice that we could slide on. We had a large, one-liter, glass bottle that we would sit on, holding on to the neck, and slide down the ramp. It was the fastest, most fabulous ride! If the bottle had broken we could have gotten badly cut, but that never crossed our minds. We wore a lot of clothes, and it never broke.

We had a lot of snow when I was growing up. Shoveling paths to the barn and the woodshed was a tiresome job, but we loved to make great big piles and then dig out the middle and make a snow cave.

Fishing and hunting

We did a lot of dangerous things. When we wanted worms for fishing we would drive a large iron spike into the ground, tie one end of a long wire to it and throw the other end over the electrical wires. We could feel the ground vibrate from the electrical current and the worms came up in droves. The chickens came running when they saw all the worms, but when they felt the vibrations they jumped back. It was quite a show! Please don't do this at home; it's very dangerous.

One day I was riding my bike down a small hill when a rabbit ran out in front of me and jumped into a ditch. I jumped off my bike and threw myself over the rabbit, catching him with my bare hands! Herbert and Paul, the neighbor's adult sons, had been out hunting rabbits all morning and hadn't caught any. They were impressed when they found out I had caught one, and I was very proud.

Ghost Stories

We heard a lot of ghost stories while we were growing up. The adults, including my father, would sit around and tell one story after the other. We thought this was extremely interesting and would sit quietly and listen.

There was a certain bridge that horses would never cross over at night. They just went wild as soon as they came close to it.

There was a woman in Skärshult who talked to her chickens and told them how far they were allowed to wander. She never fenced them in, and the chickens never crossed the line.

I don't really believe these things, but I don't like to walk past a graveyard at night, either.

We loved to run down and visit with the widow Anna, who lived about two kilometers through the forest. My father didn't like Anna; he thought she was evil, but we liked her. She talked a lot and always spoke to us as if we were grown-ups. She was really upset with the man who bought her farm after her husband died. She thought he had cheated her and she told us all about it. She said, "He is sly as a fox. He has a tail too, only his hangs in front."

She told us about a rock down by the lake. A priest named Axel had carved his initial in the rock. She claimed that every time the rock heard the church bells chime it would turn over. I went by that rock many times, but it was always lying on the same side. I guess it never heard the bells chiming!

Anna told us other stories. Once she told us about a man who walked backwards around the church seven times reciting the Lord's Prayer backwards, after which he received certain powers that allowed him to do all kinds of things. We were discerning enough not to try this, but it was fun to listen to her.

No Angel

$\mathcal{L}$innea has always claimed that I was my father's favorite child. I think I was really the compliant child, trying hard to please, and I just didn't get into so much trouble. But I wasn't quite as virtuous as I let on. Sometimes I could be pretty sneaky.

One morning I was a little late and my mother said, "Hurry up now so you don't miss the milk truck. If you do, you'll get a spanking." I knew very well that my mother would not spank me, but what about my father? Coming over the last hill before reaching the road I saw the milk truck driving away. Now what would I do? I thought, "If I hide the milk in the forest until I come home from school, I can bring it home and pretend it is the skim milk. I'll feed the calves with it and no one will know the difference."

Above: Left to right: Solveig, me,
Aunt Berta, Birgitta, and Linnea

What I didn't know was that, before I came home from school, Linnea had been down to the road and came back and told my parents that there wasn't any milk down there.

When I came home from school carrying the milk on my bicycle, my father met me in the yard and asked, "Where did you leave the milk?" I answered, "Down by the road." He asked me the same question again and received the same answer. When he asked me that question a third time I realized that I was in trouble and I told him the truth, "I hid it in the forest."

I think it's interesting that he asked me three times. Peter, after denying Christ three times, went out and cried bitterly. I, too, cried bitterly, but only because I got caught and because I got a well-deserved spanking that day.

One day I was passing by the store in Slättö and suddenly got a terrible craving for candy. We didn't get candy very often, but here I was walking right past it. My parents had an account at the store so that they could ask us to go in and pick up some yeast whenever my mother needed some. I thought to myself, "If I go in and get some yeast, I could buy a piece of candy and they would never know the difference."

It seemed like a good idea at the time, so I went in, got my candy and pocketed the yeast. I had planned to throw it in the forest on my way home, but I forgot.

Coming home, I realized that it was still in my pocket so I threw it to the chickens, thinking that they would eat anything. But, as luck would have it, my father walked passed the chicken coop just minutes later. Again he asked me, "What did you do with the yeast?" Well, I still figured that he couldn't know that I'd had the yeast, but he kept asking until I confessed - another spanking!

Although my father was a very strict disciplinarian, these are the only two times I can remember that I got spanked, and I did deserve them. I think he missed the opportunity to explain to me why we shouldn't do the things I had done and, more importantly, that it was wrong to lie. It would have been more effective, but he wasn't very good at communicating.

Sometimes I didn't get caught.

One beautiful summer day I didn't want to go to school. I packed my lunch in the morning as I usually did, and left the house. Half way to school there was an open field. I stopped there and enjoyed the day. I put a stick in the ground and drew a clock around it. With this primitive sundial I could see when it was three o'clock and time to go home. It worked perfectly, so I did it again the next day! When I came home the second day, my mother looked up and said, "Oh, here she comes. Poor thing, she has been in school all day." I felt so guilty, but I never said anything. I wonder if she knew, anyway?

We received dental care through the school. Once a year they filled a car with kids and drove us to Vrigstad, 19 kilometers away, to the local dentist. This was a big event for us. There was a small store that sold candy near the dentist's office, but we didn't have any money. Linnea and I decided to steal some money out of our parent's desk. We took a big risk. If we had been caught, we would have gotten the spanking of our lives. But we didn't get caught.

One summer day, when I was visiting my grandparents in Klerebo, I walked down the hill to the village. Outside the store there was a machine that sold candy for 10 or 25 cents. I thought that if I flattened a one-cent coin with two rocks, it would be as big as a 10-cent coin. I remember sitting by the side of the road pounding on this one-cent coin. When I thought it looked about right I went down to the machine and put it in the 10-cent slot and out came a candy. Sometimes success tastes good, but deception leaves a sour aftertaste.

Forgiven

Saliga (or Blessed) Emma was a woman who, after raising her two children and eight stepchildren, felt led by the Lord to return to Hjälmseryd and build a chapel. She was just a poor widow, but she had a vision and was filled with the joy of the Lord. She belonged to the Pentecostal Church and came to a community that was strictly Lutheran, but she found five people who joined her in prayer for a new chapel. It was 1930, the middle of the depression even in Sweden, and people didn't have much money. But when Emma came around to talk to them they would donate one crown, or five crowns. My grandfather donated a piece of land where the chapel could be built. They cleared the land and made lumber from the trees they cut down. Emma went around on her bicycle talking to people who owned building, plumbing, and electrical supplies. No one said no to her; they all donated something even though they weren't interested in joining her group.

In 1937 the new chapel was dedicated. They called it Filadelfia. It was a beautiful building that seated 250 people, and had an overflow room that sat 30 more. On the day of the dedication it was packed. In front they had a baptistery for immersion, and on the wall they wrote:

The joy of the Lord is your strength.
Nehemiah 8:10

Emma turned 75 in 1944 and there were great celebrations. She received a letter from America with a check for $10,000. This was an incredible amount of money for Emma. Her first thought was that now we could pay off the debt on the chapel. What a miracle that was! Filadelfia was debt free.

Filadelfia would become very important to our family. It was the place where we all came to know the Lord, a place for fellowship, prayer, learning, and service.

Before they call I will answer.
Isaiah 65:24

One day at a prayer meeting at Filadelfia, I opened my Bible and received this verse:

Call to me and I will answer you and tell you
great and unsearchable things you do not know.
Jeremiah 33:3

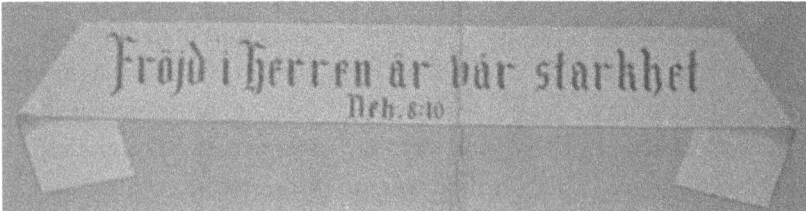

Although my parents had both been baptized and confirmed in the Lutheran church, they had never accepted Christ. Linnea had a friend in Hjälmseryd who invited her to come with her to Filadelfia, the Pentecostal church. She went, enjoyed it, and before long she had become a Christian. My parents were probably not too happy about it at the time. I remember one time they were going to play cards. My father said a little derisively, "Linnea doesn't want to play with us, she's a Christian now."

On weekends my father, his friend, Otto, and a few other friends would get together to drink. They made their own moonshine, keeping the still in our pantry. It took awhile to make, and it was a big secret because it was illegal to make your own liquor. When they got together they sat there and bragged about how good it was, "This is the best stuff ever." I actually thought it was fun when they were drinking. They were so happy, laughing and joking with us kids. They were never violent, but sometimes they drank too much and got sick. Otto was so sick one time, he lay in the bushes vomiting and crying. "Not even a woman, in the middle of labor, is as sick as I am right now."

When I was about ten years old, a revival began in Hjälmseryd and Otto went forward during the altar call and accepted the Lord. My father was pretty skeptical about the whole thing. He said he'd wait and see if Otto would still cheat. One night he went to an evening service at Filadelfia, mostly out of curiosity, I don't think he had ever been there before. At the altar call, he went forward and accepted Jesus as his savior. Soon after that my mother also came to know the Lord. They were both baptized and joined the church.

I noticed a big change in their lives. There was more joy and singing. One day my father took his deck of cards, opened the top of our wooden stove and slowly dropped the deck of cards in the fire. He sang, "Sin and world farewell forever, you will never get me back." In those days it was considered a sin to play cards, but we'll not get into the theology of that right now.

He was also addicted to snuff and quit that cold turkey.

Father read his Bible a lot. One day he came across a passage that said that you should give ten percent of your earnings to the Lord. That year he sold some forest for ten thousand crowns. At the Wednesday night prayer meeting, he put one thousand crowns into the offering plate. These are good memories.

Once in a while we held a prayer meeting in our kitchen and a few people would come. A couple of times we had a house meeting, and the whole neighborhood was invited. We set up benches in the living room. I remember my mother checking the furniture and making sure that my father's picture was in a prominent place. She thought he was so handsome and wanted everyone to see.

My mother kept this portrait of my father in a prominent place in our sitting room. She was so proud of him and thought he was very handsome.

We started going to Bible school that was held on Saturdays in Hjälmseryd. The pastor was just wonderful with kids and we loved to go there. It was seven kilometers to Hjälmseryd and we had to walk, but I wanted to go no matter how bad the weather was. One Saturday it was raining really, really hard and Father said that we couldn't go. I was so disappointed, but I knew that it was useless to argue with him.

On a cold winter night in February 1945, my best friend, Alva, and I went to a service at Filadelfia. When the service was over we began walking home. I wanted to become a Christian, so we turned around and went back, knocked on the pastor's door and said, "We want to be saved." He asked us in and prayed with us. How happily we walked the long road home! Snow lit up the road and the countryside, and in our hearts there was peace and light.

A year later I was baptized in water, and I joined the church.

Now I faced a dilemma. I believed that now, when I was a Christian and Jesus had forgiven me of all my sins, I needed to go to anyone whom I had cheated in the past and ask their forgiveness.

I am about 13 years old here, not long after I became a Christian and was baptized. As members of the Pentecostal Church we were not allowed to have short hair, so I let mine grow and rolled it up in a bun.

I started with my classmate, Elsa, from whom I had stolen 25 cents. I confessed to her and asked her to forgive me, and I gave her back the money. She was gracious enough to forgive me.

Then there was Anders, a grumpy old man who never talked to us. He owned the farm next to ours in Lindö, but he didn't live there. He lived in Karshult. Everyday he would walk to his farm. I had stolen apples from his farm and felt that I should ask his forgiveness. This was especially hard for me because I was so shy and hardly ever spoke to anyone outside my own family, but one day I forced myself to catch up with him when he walked by. I asked him to forgive me for stealing his apples. He was quite friendly. He said, "I've always admired you children because you haven't taken very much from my farm." He wasn't as scary as I feared, just a little grumpy. But I was still too shy to ever speak to him again.

The last person on my list was my mother. I decided to write a note and leave it on her bed where she couldn't miss it. We all slept in the same room, so when she came up I pretended to be asleep. The note read:

Mamma,

> *I stole some money from you when we went to the dentist. Would you forgive me?*

> *_____yes   _____no*

I knew she was crying because I could hear her sniffling. In the morning I found the note. She had marked it, "yes." We never spoke of it at all, but I knew I was forgiven.

Miracles

Although my father was rather strict and gruff, he had a gentle side that would occasionally reveal itself. One year, the day before Mother's Day, he said to me, "Let's get up early and take care of the barn tomorrow, do the milking and feed the animals. That way your mother can sleep in." This didn't happen very often and I thought it was a good idea, but how would I wake up? I didn't want to ask my father to wake me up so I prayed, "Dear Lord, help me to wake up at seven o'clock tomorrow morning." Early the next morning a small bird pecked at my window and woke me up. It was exactly seven o'clock. What a God we serve!

I was at a prayer meeting at our pastor's house when I was about 14 years old. We knelt, like we usually did, and suddenly I felt the presence of the Lord so powerfully my body began to shake. I was too shy to tell anyone about it, but I felt so full of joy because God was so good to me. I still felt that overwhelming joy the next day. I was running out to the field where we were working that day, praising God like the crippled man that had been healed by Peter.

*He went into
the temple courts,
walking and leaping
and praising God.
Acts 2:49*

One Saturday every spring the women got together at Filadelfia and we would scrub the wood floors in the sanctuary. We did this on our hands and knees and it took all day. Afterwards we had a prayer meeting. That was one time I thought it was fun to work without pay.

One winter night I drove the horse and sleigh home from Filadelfia by myself. Gliding quietly over the snow-packed roads beneath the starry sky, I was filled with the joy of the Lord and sang all the way home.

Whiter than snow, whiter than snow
Clean me in the blood of Jesus
Then I will be whiter than snow

By the time I came home to Lindö my legs had fallen asleep. I had to sit there and wait for them to regain some feeling before I could unharness the horse.

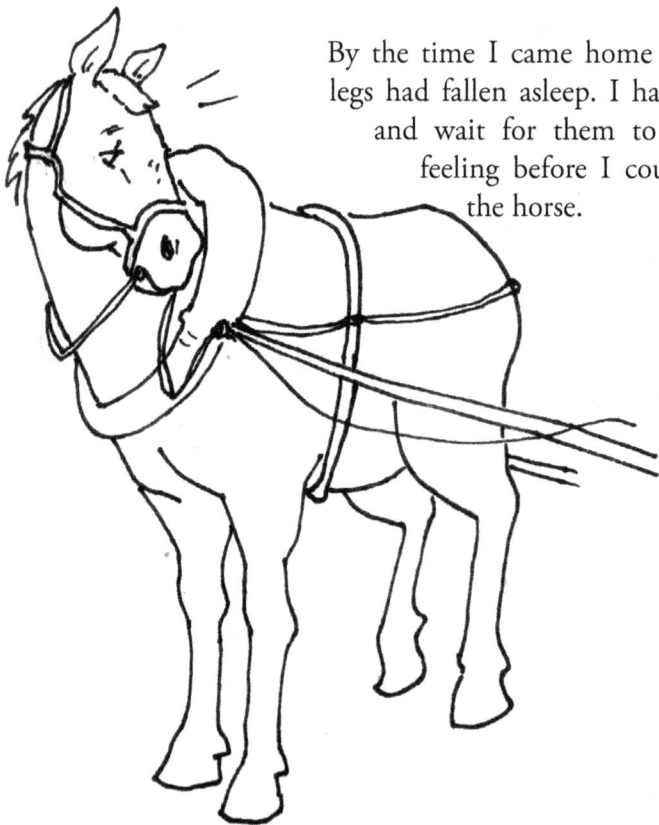

On My Own

In 1946 I graduated from sixth grade and my formal schooling was complete. My father gave me a Bible and a bicycle. I would be 14 years old in August and was now expected to begin working. With my bicycle, a small suitcase and a guitar I was ready to head out into the world.

It was exciting to set out on my own. I found a job in a family that had four or five kids. They lived on a farm, and I did pretty much the same things I had done at home, only now I got paid. I worked for them over the summer.

In the fall I came home and went to something called, "Continuation School." I don't really remember what we studied, but I think it was a bit of a review, and then the girls were taught cooking and sewing, while the boys learned carpentry. Continuation School was held for six weeks in the fall, the first two years after the completion of sixth grade.

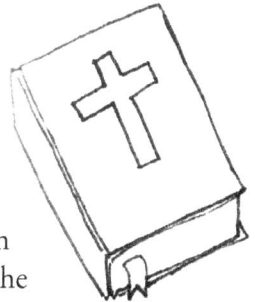

Left to right: Birgitta, Linnea, Ove, me holding Yvonne, Solveig

Yvonne

I was offered a job as a seamstress at a clothes factory in Rörvik. I rented a room in town and started working. I was a quick learner, and they said I was a very good seamstress. My mother was expecting another baby and wanted me to be at home when she was due to deliver, so, a little grudgingly, I came home. I remember a certain bitterness that there always had to be a kid on the way.

My sister, Yvonne, was born in October 1947. Eventually, when things at home returned to normal, I returned to Rörvik and my job at the factory.

Bicycle Trip

In the summer of 1948 I was 15 years old. My friend, Iris, and I decided to bicycle to Öland, an island on the east coast of Sweden. It was a long trip, 164 km to Kalmar where we caught the ferry. Then we continued 85 km to the northern part of the island, where we camped at a campground for a week. And then we had to bicycle home again!

Uncle Oskar

In 1948 my father's brother, Uncle Oskar, came to visit from America. He wore the big, flashy, colorful ties that were so in style at the time. I thought he was so elegant, and I thought that wherever it was that Uncle Oskar lived, that is where I wanted to go. My cousin, Ruth, who was the same age as me, was also interested in seeing the states. We talked to Uncle Oskar, who agreed to sponsor us, and went out and got our passports. But Ruth's mother didn't want her to go, and

I didn't want to go by myself, so the whole plan fell through. As things turned out, it was probably just as well.

I continued working at the factory until the summer of '49, when I decided to quit and take a job in a family. Once again I was on a farm, helping the farmer's wife who had just given birth to her second child.

105

It was a good summer for me. I rode my bike to the tent meetings in Rörvik as often as I could. I was so happy and thankful that Jesus had saved me. One afternoon I was standing in the kitchen washing dishes, quietly praying and thanking God, when suddenly my prayers were no longer in Swedish. I was baptized in the Holy Spirit right there by the kitchen sink, praying in a language unknown to me. The Lord surprised me that day and gave me a new prayer language, a language I have used ever since. I was full of joy and thankfulness.

I have told you this so that my joy may be in you
and that your joy may be complete.
John 15:11

Linnea's wedding

My sister, Linnea, got married in May 1950. She had known Helge for a few years and the whole family really liked him. He was a carpenter and they had built a house in Hjälmseryd where they were going to live. I was the maid of honor and Helge's brother, Erik, was the best man. The four of us went to the priest in Hjälmseryd and they were married. It was just a quiet ceremony, but friends and family were waiting to celebrate the newlyweds when we returned to Lindö. When we took pictures Erik squeezed my hand. I was 17 and I thought it was so exciting. No man had ever squeezed my hand before.

My mother cried that day, not because Linnea was getting married, but because she realized that she was pregnant again. Forty-five years old, with

six children already, it's understandable that she really didn't want to have any more.

In the fall I started going to nursing school. It was a one-year course and when I was finished I would be a practical nurse and would be able to care for people in their homes. But I never finished, because once again, I was called home.

Joy and Sorrow

My mother, who was eight months pregnant, had been writing to me to please come home. My father had been ill for some time, losing weight and so weak he could not stand up or even lift a pitcher of milk off the table. When I came home in January '51, he was in the hospital. I believe he had Addison's disease, although they didn't call it that at the time. They said there was a problem with the adrenal glands. I remember that he was sick for a long time, in and out of the hospital. I really had no other choice, so I quit school and went home.

Leaving me at home to run the farm and care for the younger children, my mother took the bus to the hospital in Jönköping, where she would remain until the baby was born. Kurt arrived on February 12th. Although the pregnancy had been unexpected and unwanted, the baby was not. Kurt was so dear and sweet, she loved him and welcomed him as much as she had all of her other children. I still have the letters she wrote to me telling me how wonderful and sweet he was.

Linnea, who was also expecting, gave birth to a little girl, Els-Marie, 14 days later.

With both of our parents in the hospital, I had a lot of responsibility and a lot to do. Birgitta and Solveig did their share when they came home from school. Ove and Yvonne were still small.

Even when Mother came home, she was still not strong and needed a lot of rest. I took care of Kurt at night, letting him sleep in a box by my bed. Before we went upstairs I would heat milk for his bottle, making it much too hot. Wrapped in a towel, the bottle would cool slowly, and by two o'clock would be the right temperature. He was a good baby. After his two o'clock feeding he would sleep till morning.

By early summer both Father and Mother were home and seemed to be feeling better and getting stronger. I thought I should get out and get a job. I wish now that I had stayed at home and helped them through the summer, but I was restless and wanted to get out on my own.

I found a job in Husqvarna, in a home for the elderly. I really liked my job but in August my mother was writing to me again and asking me to come home. My father's illness had worsened and he was hospitalized again. Normally a big

This is one of the last pictures I have of my mother. From the left: Sven, Ove, Linnea holding Els-Marie, Solveig, Birgitta, Yvonne, Father holding Kurt, and Mother.

man, he had lost so much weight he now weighed around 100 pounds. We feared for his life.

At the same time my mother was having severe stomach pains; we didn't understand how severe. When the doctors recommended surgery, she felt that she had no other choice. I wonder, though, if she didn't have a premonition. She was anxious and worried, talking aloud to herself about her concerns. Just before leaving for the hospital she gathered all of us in the living room to pray. She cried out to the Lord, "How can I leave my little ones?"

Mother went to the hospital in Värnamo where she was scheduled for testing. They were long days, and she wrote several letters telling me how lonely it was, and how she missed the little ones. I still have her letters and I read them to my siblings when we were all together a couple of years ago.

Surgery was scheduled for the end of October. They thought they were going to repair an ulcer, but when they opened her up they discovered her gallbladder was inflamed and she had gallstones. She must have been in severe pain, more pain than we realized. They decided to remove the gallstones and take care of the ulcer at a later date. I suppose taking care of both problems would have been too complicated.

After surgery she didn't recover as expected; her body was shutting down. We took turns sitting by her bedside. My father was still very ill, prognosis unsure, and he was in the same hospital. I was sitting with my mother when they brought him to see her. He bent over her and said, "I have not always understood you. Would you please forgive me?" She said, "Ja, ja, we must forgive each other."

Later that night, November 7, 1951, her condition worsened. She was talking a lot and she was very thirsty. She said, "Soon I will drink of the living water, I can hear the sound of it now." Her last words were, "Now I see Jesus!" The room was filled with peace, a peace I can't explain. This is a bright and glorious memory from the saddest day of my life.

My father was still deathly ill. He said later, "I knew that one of us was going to die. I just thought it would be me."

He had six children at home; the youngest was only eight months old. He must have been terribly anxious about all of us.

Sorrow is like a fog that isolates you from everyone and everything, except your own pain. Memories from the days following my mother's death are mostly hazy, with occasional glimpses of clarity. My father was released from the hospital and came home, but he was still very weak. Linnea from Linnevik, my mother's cousin, came to Lindö and stayed, helping us to sew the black mourning clothes we had to wear. She was so wonderful, telling us stories as she sewed. She stayed for several days, helping us get through each day and keeping our minds off what had happened.

On the day of the funeral, the one thing that is vivid in my memory is the hearse coming down the road to Lindö. Arriving at the farm, they opened the coffin so that we could view the body of our mother one last time. Then we loaded up the car and followed the hearse to the graveyard in Hjälmseryd. Father was still so weak that he had to sit in a chair at the grave side service.

We were not a physical family; we didn't hug or kiss, in fact we hardly touched each other, except when we siblings were fighting. A few days after the funeral, my father broke down and cried at the dinner table. We just sat there and waited for the storm to pass. No one got up to comfort him with a hug, or even a pat on the shoulder. It just wasn't done in our family.

We wore black, according to custom, for six months. We girls also wore black veils when we went out. After six months we wore a black armband over our normal clothes to show that we were still in mourning. A year after my mother's death we abandoned the outward signs of mourning. In our hearts, of course, we would never quite get over her loss.

America Bound

America Bound

$\mathcal{L}$innea and I decided that we should learn how to drive. I rode my bicycle seven kilometers to Linnea's house, and then we rode her little motorcycle ten kilometers to the driving school in Lammhult. We were afraid of the police, since we didn't have a license to drive the motorcycle either, so we parked outside of town and walked to the school.

Driving school was a lot of fun. We learned to drive with manual transmission, and we laughed till we cried as we jerked and jumped along the road. They were still driving on the left side of the road in the 50's but the steering wheels were mounted on the left side. Of course this made driving, and especially passing other cars, tricky, not to mention dangerous. We, of course, didn't know any difference. It wasn't until I came to America that I realized

Above: At 18 My hair is still long and rolled into a bun
in accordance to the rules of the Pentecostal Church

how much easier it was to drive a left-steered car on the right side of the road.

We had to learn how to drive in city traffic, so our teacher took us to Växjö. Then he took us out to lunch. At 18 and 22, we had not been to many restaurants and we were lost! We didn't know how to act in a restaurant.

We learned to drive, took the test, and passed the first time, receiving our driver's licenses.

Going to America

After my mother died I stayed home for a year and a half to help my father with the farm and the smaller children. I had given up my dream of becoming a nurse, but my dreams of America were alive and becoming more intense. Kurt was two and a half years old; I thought someone else could take over. My immigration papers were ready; my plane ticket was purchased. I was ready for new adventures. When I think back, I realize how wrong I was, as they still needed a lot of help. I feel guilty that I didn't stay, but they all grew up; they all become productive citizens, and, thank God, they are all Christians.

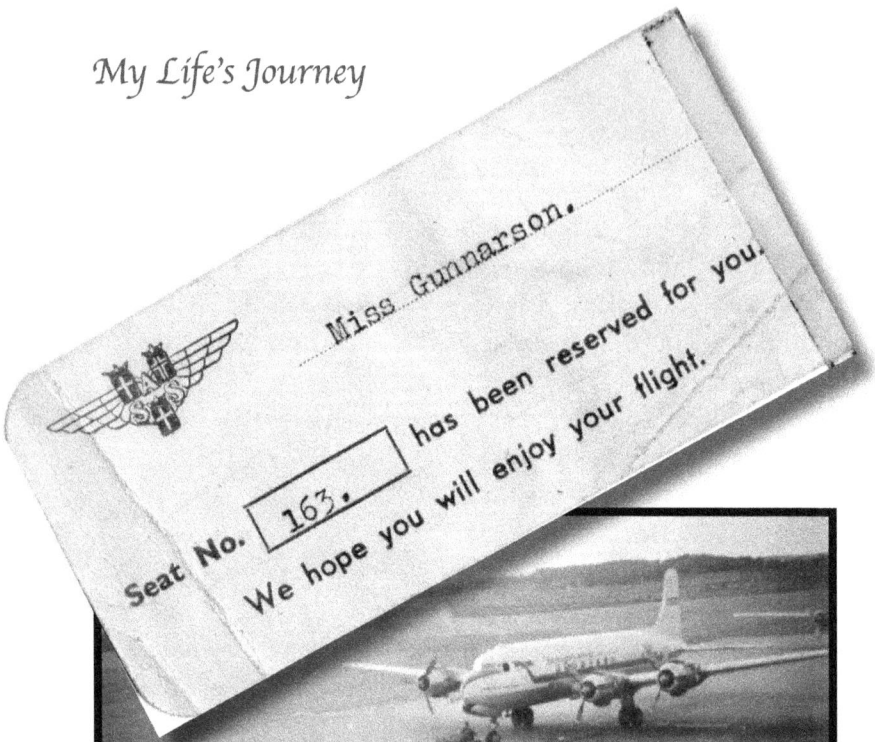

116

Air travel was new and exciting in 1953. Most people still crossed the Atlantic by ship, but for some reason, I don't remember why, I chose to fly. Perhaps I was in a hurry to get there. One guy, who was very fond of me, found out what airplane I was leaving on and followed me to Stockholm to see me off. It was a little embarrassing since I didn't feel as strongly for him as he felt for me.

I wasn't at all nervous about flying. It was a small plane by today's standards and we had to stop somewhere to refuel, I don't remember where. I do remember that I was terribly nervous about coming through customs and immigration in New York. I asked the steward what they would do to me when I got there. He had a good sense of humor and made some jokes about it, which made me feel that, perhaps, it wouldn't be so scary after all. When we landed we were all given a certificate for crossing the Atlantic, following the old Norse Vikings in the new ships of the air, endowing us with the title, "Viking of the Air." And, just as the steward had said, customs was a piece of cake!

The first thing that impressed me about New York were the cars, there were so many! I had friends who picked me up at the airport, and we drove out on the freeways and around the city. I had never seen so many cars. I still love looking at the 50's cars. There were tall skyscrapers, and people everywhere, people living on top of each other. For a girl who had grown up on a small farm, in the middle of the forest, at the end of the world, New York was a busy, bustling, throbbing metropolis. We went to the Empire State Building and to Coney Island. Everywhere we went it was crowded, and I loved it!

117

I wasn't staying in New York though; I was headed for Rockford, Illinois. My friends took me to the Greyhound bus station and helped me buy a ticket to Rockford. I had to transfer in Chicago, and I didn't speak any English, so I asked my friends to write a note that I could take to the information desk, asking where to catch the bus to Rockford.

I had a two or three hour wait in Chicago's enormous bus station. Sitting there, afraid to take my eyes off the gate, I felt so alone. I used to be so shy that I wouldn't talk. Now, when I desperately needed someone to talk to, I couldn't. A few minutes later I spotted a man sitting near me, reading a Swedish newspaper. I was so relieved. We started talking, and he assured me that I was in the right place and all I had to do was wait for the bus.

When I arrived in Rockford, my sponsor, Pastor Erik Peterson, was waiting for me. Erik was from Rörvik but lived with his family in Rockford. Visiting Sweden in 1951, he came to the hospital to visit my mother. I was sitting by her bedside. Knowing of my desire to come to America, he offered to sponsor me if I ever decided to come over. He and his family were very nice and helpful. I stayed with them for a few days. They helped me to apply for a Social Security Number so that I could begin looking for work. I also took the driver's test and got my American driver's license.

My sponsor, Erik Peterson, his wife, and five of their ten children.

My first job in Rockford was in a screw factory. It was June and, since there was no air-conditioning, it was hot and tedious. I really didn't like working there, but it was a job, and I was learning to speak English. In the 1950's Rockford was 75% Swedish. I rented a room from some nice people, Swedish decedents, who treated me like a daughter, and I started taking evening classes in English.

Restless by nature, it didn't take long until Rockford began to seem small. I found a job working in a family with two children. The job was only for three months, January to March, but they were going to Phoenix, Arizona. That was exciting, I wanted to see more of the country and I had nothing against spending the winter months someplace warm. Our Swedish-American pastor in Chicago, Mattson Boze (pictured left), was hired to drive me and a few other servants to Arizona in the family's Cadillac. He was good company, and we talked a lot. I was so excited just to be traveling again. I'll never forget when we came to Phoenix and I saw palm trees and orange trees for the first time. I thought Phoenix was the most wonderful place I had ever seen.

Astrid Eriksson, Belgian Kongo

One day I was shopping in Phoenix when Astrid Eriksson came to my mind. Astrid was a missionary in Afrika that our church in Sweden was supporting. I felt that I should buy her some stockings, underwear and a blouse. I purchased seven pairs of stockings and a few other things and mailed them to her. She told me later that she'd had only one pair of stockings left and the Lord had told her to give them to a fellow worker who needed a pair. She had argued with the Lord, "It's my last pair, Lord." But He had said to give them away, so she did. A week letter my package arrived. It's exciting to see how the Lord works, and an incredible blessing to have been used by Him.

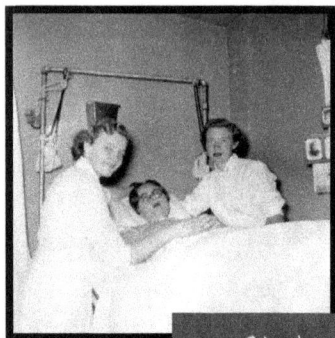

She is a heart.
Nobody is like her.

When the three months were over so was my job and we returned to Chicago. I rented a room in the city and got a job at the Swedish Covenant Hospital as a nurse's aid. I liked the job, but was already planning on moving on. I met another Swedish girl, Vivianne. We worked well together and became friends. (Fifty-four years later, Vivianne and I are still friends.) She was homesick and was planning on going back to Sweden as soon as she had saved up enough money. As we became better friends though, she began to change her mind and we made plans to go to California together.

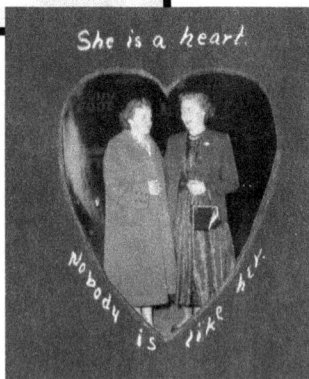

Not having much money, we didn't know how we would get there, but then I saw an ad in the newspaper. This company was looking for drivers to transport cars from Chicago to different parts of the country. It sounded good to me, so I called them. They had a car, a small Nash, which needed to be delivered to Visalia, California. It's rather amazing that they would trust me, a young, foreign girl, with the responsibility of driving someone else's car.

Another Swedish friend, Gunhild, asked if she could go with us, so now we were three, but I was the only one with a driver's license. Having a third person along helped with expenses. Although the car was free and so was a portion of the gasoline, we still had to pay for hotel rooms along the way. I was young and enjoyed driving; I could drive for hours. When I got tired we would stop for a bite to eat, or we'd find a hotel and get a room for the three of us.

We had a wonderful time traveling across the country. Driving through Salt Lake City, we stopped to see the Mormon Temple. The only thing we knew about Mormons was that they had several wives. We were a little concerned that they might kidnap us and take us as an extra wife. Yes, we were naïve.

California Here We come!

We had to keep going because we had to deliver the car by a certain date, so the next day we were on our way again, headed towards Los Angeles. I'll never forget when we got to the border and saw the sign:

WELCOME TO
CALIFORNIA!

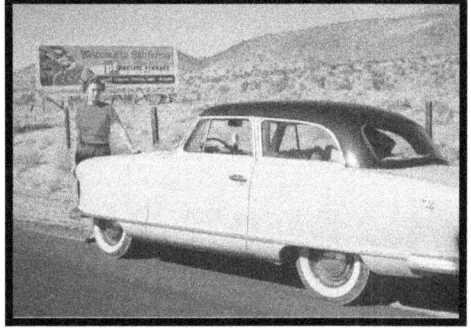

Arriving in Los Angeles, we had to find a room to rent, leave our things and then drive to Visalia to deliver the car. Having done that, we took a bus back to Los Angeles. Before long we had each found jobs working for rich families in Beverly Hills. I was hired to take care of Tyrone Power's mother. Every day when I came to work, she would ask, "Do you know who I am? I am Tyrone Power's mother." Vivianne worked as a personal assistant to the actress, Vanessa Brown, and got to travel with her on an airplane, and Gunhild worked for Judy Garland, who spent her days crying in her bedroom and her evenings partying in Hollywood.

I was still not very proficient in English. I remember once, when I was working for the Cook family in Beverly Hills, that I had to write the laundry list. I wrote:

4 pillowcases
2 shits (sheets)

I didn't understand at the time why Mrs. Cook found that so amusing!

We had Thursdays and Sundays off. On Thursdays I took the bus Park La Brea and cleaned two apartments. The extra money was a welcome addition as I was saving every penny I could. Pretty soon I had enough to buy my own car!

We didn't know anyone in Los Angeles when we arrived, but Pastor Mattson Boze, in Chicago, had given us the name of a Swedish Church that we should visit. Immanuel Christian Assembly had a congregation that was about 75% Swedish. We got to know so many people, both young and old. It was a real blessing for us. The pastor, Paul Zettersten, was also from Sweden. He was a good teacher, preached mostly in English, and we really enjoyed listening to him.

We were a group of young people in the church that hung around together. I dated a few of the young men. One young man from Sweden, Ted, was my steady boyfriend for a few months. He took me to my very first Rose Parade and we had a lot of fun together, but I realized after awhile that he was not Mr. Right and broke off the relationship. We remained friends though. He wrote me a card:

Thank you for the roses along the way
That is what the song says
You are a rose that I found along life's path
That has given me much happiness

We had heard about another church, Angeles Temple, which we decided we wanted to visit. Looking at the map we saw that it was close enough for us to walk to, but there was a big road we would have to cross. We followed a long ramp up to the busy road that had no crosswalks. Not easily deterred, we waited for an opening in the traffic and then ran across. We didn't know it at the time, but that big road we crossed was the Harbor freeway. We must have had angels watching over us that day!

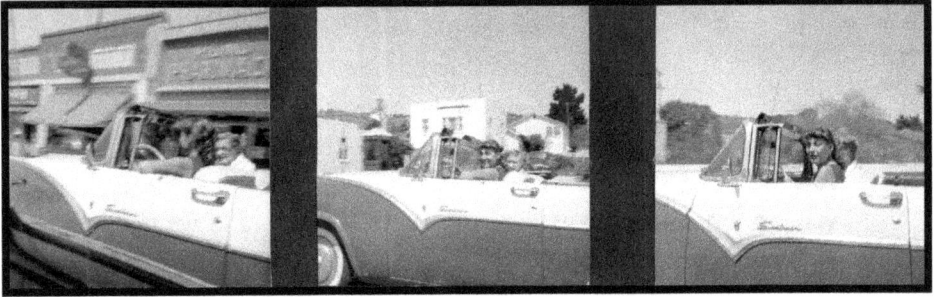

I Found Love on Hwy 101

In 1955 I met a girl from Austria. Melitta had a job selling magazines, and told me that she would train me and we could be a team. She had a red and white Ford Fairlane Convertible and traveled a lot with her job. We were actually a team of ten people, but Melitta and I drove together in her car, meeting up with the group in predetermined cities.

On April 22nd, we were driving up Highway 101. A car with two young men was stopped at a stop sign at the crossroad to Solvang. The young men noticed us, two girls in a convertible, and set after us in hot pursuit. We drove fast in those days, 80 m.p.h., and to pass you had to go even faster. Once they had passed us they slowed down and let us pass them, then sped up and passed us again. This went on for a while. They even took pictures of us; I still have the pictures Orla took of us before we even met. We came to a town and had to slow down. Driving up next to us, the guys rolled down their window and asked if we wanted to stop for refreshments.

Not wanting to appear too easy, we told them no. But Melitta said, "Let's stop at a gas station and see if they follow us." They did and we soon found out that we had something in common. We were all foreigners, Orla and John from Denmark, Melitta from Austria and I, from Sweden. We decided to have coffee at a coffee shop, and sat there talking for two or three hours. They had jukeboxes at every table, the kind you can see today at nostalgic diners. I can remember that someone at another table, played the song, "Why do Fools Fall in Love?" And Orla said, "Yeah, why do they?"

We made arrangements to meet again the following week at a restaurant in San Francisco. Little did I know, it would change the entire course of my life.

I liked Orla, but he liked Melitta, so we left it at that. They drove back to Sacramento where they both lived and worked. Melitta and I continued on our tour up the coast, stopping at different cities along the way to meet with the rest of the team. We went all the way to Seattle, where we turned around and headed south again.

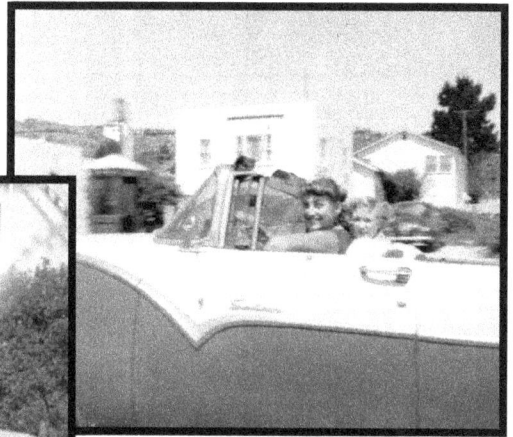

On our way back through Sacramento, we decided to call Orla and John. We double dated a few times. Orla, deciding that he liked me best after all, gave me a picture of himself. I kept that picture on my nightstand, not knowing if we would ever meet again, but hoping!

Melitta and I continued on our way to Los Angeles.

I had decided that it was time for me to return to Sweden so I booked passage on the M/S Stockholm, leaving New York on July 25, 1956. I had a car, a '55 Plymouth, painted in two shades of green that I thought was so pretty, and decided I would drive to New York. I had done well in my job selling magazines, winning a prize for best salesperson in our group. The prize was a check for $700, issued by a bank in Chicago. I didn't have time to wait the two weeks for the check to clear, so I decided I would cash it when I drove through Chicago on my way to the east coast.

1955 Plymouth that I bought with the hard earned money I saved. I drove this car to New York and later brought it with me to Sweden.

My sister, Solveig, who had come to Los Angeles ten months earlier when she was 16, decided she would go with me part of the way. Our mother's Uncle Solomon, who lived in San Francisco, wanted to visit his relatives in Denver and wondered if he could get a ride with us. They were our relatives too, so we thought that would be fun. We drove to San Francisco to pick him up.

I called Orla before we left San Francisco, thinking that we could meet one last time. His sister, Birgitte, answered, and when I asked for him said, "Just a minute, I'll get him."

She came back after a couple of minutes and said, "Oh, he just left."

Well, I figured that he just didn't want to talk to me and had told her to tell me he wasn't there. I buried his picture at the bottom of my suitcase.

Disappointed, I left San Francisco with my uncle and my sister. We stopped in Utah to go swimming in Salt Lake. That was a weird experience; the salt water makes you so buoyant. Uncle Solomon, who couldn't swim, just sat on the water and laughed his heart out!

We stayed with our relatives in Denver. They were so nice and we had a really good time. After a few days, I continued on to New York by myself. Uncle Solomon was staying on in Denver for a while, and Solveig took the bus back to Los Angeles. I didn't worry about her; she had been in the country for almost a year and could take care of herself. That is at least how we felt at the time. Looking back, I am amazed and almost fearful for the young girl, only 16 when she immigrated and 17 when I left her alone in Los Angeles. She did survive, but when I think of all the things that could have happened......

Alone in the car, my thoughts turned back to Orla and a love lost.

It only hurts for a little while
That's what they tell me
That's what they say

Singing that song to give myself courage to continue, I drove on towards Rockford, Illinois. I wanted to visit Erik Petersson and his family before going home. Uncle Oskar was living in Chicago at the time so I spent the night with him and his wife, cashed my check at the bank on Clark Street, and hit the road again.

I needed to get to Brooklyn, to my friends who had picked me up at the airport when I first arrived. Driving through that big city, with all the traffic, I searched for their apartment. Of course, I didn't know the city or even recognize more than a few landmarks, my stay in New York having been so short and everything had been so new and overwhelming when I had just arrived in this country. Eventually, reading the map as I drove, I found them.

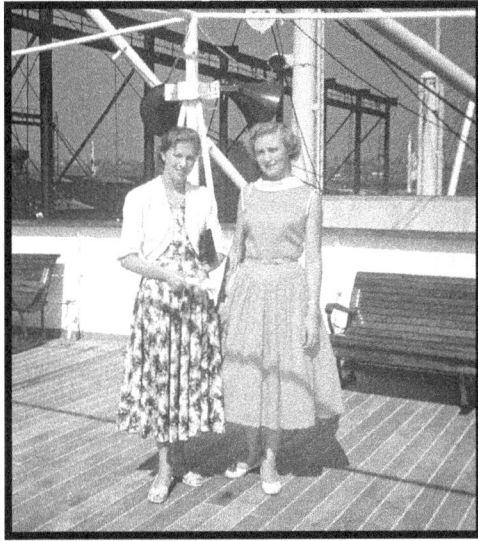

Shipwrecked!

On the 25th of July I left my car with my friends, who had agreed to sell it for me, and boarded the M/S Stockholm bound for Gothenburg, Sweden. I had never been on a ship before and it was quite impressive. My cabin was located on the lower levels, near the bow of the ship. Coming in, the first thing I noticed was the letter sitting on my nightstand. It was from Orla.

I had been mistaken; he was still interested! When I called that day and spoke with his sister, he had just left on a trip to the mountains. But he might have forgotten about me had it not been for Melitta. Still traveling with the magazine, she looked him up while passing through Sacramento, and just happened to mention that I was going back to Sweden aboard the Stockholm and that I really liked him. Encouraged, he wrote me a letter.

Tearing open the letter, I sat on my bed and read through it quickly once, and then again slowly, savoring each word. My skin prickled and my heart fluttered with joy. I dug his picture out from the bottom of my suitcase and stood it on my nightstand and just gazed at his handsome face. Everything was right with the world.

I stood on deck as we eased away from the dock, waving to my friends among the crowd. Streamers and confetti filled the air along with a chorus of "Good-by," "Good Luck," and "Bon Voyage!"

During dinner the steward informed us of the activities available on board, lounges for coffee and other stimulants, dancing, games, beauty parlors, shops and movie theaters. A safety drill, he informed us, would be held in the morning, at which time they would tell us where our life jackets were located and how to get to the lifeboats.

It was terribly foggy that night, not one for moonlit strolls on deck, so I decided to watch a movie. I don't remember what was playing. It probably didn't matter; I was so filled with thoughts of Orla that I probably wouldn't have noticed if it were a love story or a horror movie.

At 11:10 that night I was back in my cabin, dressed in my nightgown, brushing my teeth. Suddenly there was a loud crash and I was knocked off my feet. The air was filled with smoke and dust. My first thought was that we had hit an iceberg, but no, there aren't any icebergs outside of New York.

I took the first stairwell I could find and ran up to the deck. I met a steward who told me to go back and put on my life jacket. I didn't know where it was; we hadn't had the safety drill yet! I ran back to my cabin, found my life jacket, put it on and ran back out on deck.

There was debris everywhere; foghorns were blowing, people were screaming; a few men who had been pulled from the debris lay injured on deck, one with his legs mangled and twisted. I stood there in shock observing the scene. How quickly our peaceful evening at sea had turned into a chaotic nightmare!

It seemed like an eternity until we could hear Captain Gunnar Nordenson's voice over the loudspeaker. We had collided with another ship, the Andrea Doria, he told us. We were not in immediate danger, and he asked that we remain calm and keep our life jackets on. A steward came up to me and told me that this area of the boat was off limits for passengers, it was too dangerous. I had taken the first stairwell I could find and ended up on what was left of the bow.

The Andrea Doria was an Italian luxury liner. Like the Titanic, it was the largest, fastest and safest ocean liner of its time. It had eleven compartments, two of which could fill with water and the ship would still stay afloat, and was considered to be unsinkable.

On July 25th, the Andrea Doria, with 1,706 souls on board, was nearing its destination, New York. Passengers and crew were celebrating their last evening on board with a Grand Ball. The Stockholm, coming out of New York, had just entered a thick fog bank when they spotted another ship on their radar. The rules of the ocean way dictated that ships passing in fog should both veer to the right, thus widening the space between them. The Stockholm veered right but, for some reason, the Andrea Doria veered left, closing the circle and the Stockholm rammed into the side of the Andrea Doria, tearing open seven of its eleven compartments.

In less than an hour the unsinkable liner was listing dangerously. Sending out an SOS, they asked the Stockholm to come and pick up their passengers.

The Stockholm answered that they, too, were severely damaged, the bow was pressed in and the number one hold had filled with water. There was one bulkhead still intact; if it broke we would also sink. They needed to maintain their present position, but if the Andrea Doria put their passengers in lifeboats, the Stockholm would pick them up.

Mangled bow of the Stockholm.

The Andrea Doria listing badly after she was struck by the Stockholm. Half of the lifeboats are still on board and unusable. (Image from USCG)

Fifteen minutes later, the Andrea Doria sent another message,

"WE ARE HEELING OVER TOO MUCH. IMPOSSIBLE TO PUT OUR BOATS OVERBOARD. PLEASE SEND LIFEBOATS IMMEDIATELY."

Captain Nordenson, the captain of the Stockholm, determined that we were not in immediate danger and ordered the lifeboats lowered. He notified his passengers over the loudspeakers that they should remain calm; the lifeboats were being lowered, not for them, but to pick up passengers from the other ship.

The Stockholm, already carrying a full load with 535 passengers and 213 crew members, rescued 570 passengers from the Andrea Doria. A French liner, the Ile de France, and other ships in the area, having heard the SOS, arrived shortly to rescue the remaining people.

On board the Stockholm a young girl, 14 years old, was found lying among the debris on the bow. Speaking only Spanish, she was crying for her mother. One of the crew members answered, "We'll find your mother." They searched diligently among the debris that had once been the bow of their ship, but could not find the woman.

In the infirmary the girl was able to give her name, Linda Morgan, and the name of her mother, Jane Cianfarra. Neither of those names appeared on Stockholm's passenger lists. It was a mystery until Linda told them she had been aboard the Andrea Doria. She had been scooped up by the Stockholm when the two ships collided. Miraculously she sustained only minor injuries. Her mother was later found among the survivors, but her stepfather and half-sister had both been killed.

In 2004 I met a couple that had been on board the Andrea Doria that night. They had met on the voyage and spent the last evening dancing together. When the ships collided they rushed out on deck. Climbing down to the waiting lifeboat, still dressed in her ball gown, she fainted and fell into the water. Strong arms pulled her into the lifeboat and as she regained consciousness she gazed into the eyes of her cavalier. One year later they were married. When their daughter was born they named her Doria in remembrance of that incredible voyage.

At nine o'clock in the morning all the survivors had been picked up. The last lifeboat, full of Andre Doria's crew members, was waiting to leave the sinking ship. Captain Calamai, wishing to go down with his ship, told them to leave without him. One of the crew members climbed back on board. "Sir," he said, "if you don't come, we will all come back on board." Reluctantly, the captain of Andrea Doria climbed down the ropes to the lifeboat, very, very sad. He never accepted another command and lived the rest of his life, his daughter said, "as if he were mourning the loss of a son."

I stayed on deck the entire night, watching as more and more survivors arrived with the lifeboats, their fancy ball gowns and tuxedos now covered in oil, and soaked in blood and water. Sometime during the early morning hours helicopters arrived to take four injured crew members and a little girl with a head injury to the hospital. I was thankful that I was not among the injured, and that our ship was still afloat

Photographer: Harry Trask, Courtesy of The Mariner's Museum.

At 9:45 the Andrea Doria, which had been lying on her side for nearly eleven hours, began to go down. Less than half an hour later, she was gone, disappearing below the waves at 10:09, almost exactly eleven hours after the collision.

On board the Stockholm, five crew members were killed in their bunks, located in the bow of the ship, and two crew members died later from injuries sustained in the collision. Forty-six people aboard the Andrea Doria were killed, the majority of them died at the time of the collision. Two passengers died as a result of injuries sustained during rescue. One four-year-old child died after sustaining head injuries when her father dropped her into the lifeboat. Another passenger, having worked diligently to save other passengers, suffered a heart attack and died on the deck of the Stockholm.

The sinking of the Andrea Doria is one of the more famous maritime disasters in history. She was also the last ocean liner to go down before air travel made the industry nearly obsolete.

Sinking in relatively shallow water, she lies at only 165 meters depth, accessible for divers, and has become a popular shipwreck to explore. In 1984 a dive team recovered the ship's safe. Thinking that it was full of valuables from the many wealthy passengers on board, they broadcasted live on television the opening of the safe, only to find that it was full of papers and documents, worthless after so many years.

The Stockholm, accompanied by a fleet of tugboats, limped back into the New York harbor. It would take months of repairs, and two million dollars, before she would sail again.

My friends from Brooklyn were waiting for me when we came in, and took me home with them to recover. We went to Rock Church, a large church in the middle of New York City, the following Sunday, and I was recognized as a survivor of the shipwreck.

Anxious to accommodate of all of their passengers, the Swedish-American line arranged passage on other liners for anyone still wishing to travel by sea. We were also allowed to bring anything we wanted. I booked passage on a Norwegian liner, the Bergensfjord. Since my friends had not had time to sell my car I decided to bring it with me, and was allowed to do so without any cost.

Home Again

Our ship docked in Bergen, Norway and, when my car had been unloaded, I began the long drive home to Småland. I was anxious to get home to the farm and see my father and the little ones. Kurt was five years old. He didn't really remember me, but Yvonne, who was nine, says she remembers the day I arrived. Walking home through the forest with Father, they came around the barn and saw my big American car parked in front of the house. When she saw me come out of the house she says, "It was like an angel came to visit us."

I suppose, coming from America, I may have had an other-worldliness about me, but that soon wore off. I had come home to help them and I quickly fell into the routines of home; cooking, cleaning, mending clothes and minding the children. Yvonne soon realized that I was no angel.

There were fewer animals, and, now when there were fewer people at home, we grew less grain, potatoes and vegetables, so I didn't need to work in the barn or in the fields.

138

In the fall I decided to take a month-long class at a Bible school in Stockholm. I thought it would be a good experience for Kurt to visit the city, so I brought him along and arranged for him to stay with some friends of mine who had also had a little boy. Although I didn't stay there myself, I came to visit often. He quickly adapted to city life; abandoning his shyness, he became very outgoing, and even acquired a Stockholm dialect.

Deciding to stay in the city for another month after I finished my class, I found a job at a big department store. I wanted to make some money before we went home for Christmas.

I stayed on the farm throughout the spring, helping out as much as I could, but, already restless, I began making plans to travel through Europe.

Orla heard about the accident, and knew that all the passengers on board the Stockholm had survived, but didn't hear anything from me for nearly a month when he received the letter I wrote when I came home. He wrote back immediately, happy to hear from me. That was encouraging; apparently he liked me! I thought that if I told him how long I was planning on staying in Sweden he would lose interest,

so I told him I was going to stay for Christmas. Then I wrote and told him that friends had invited me to go skiing in Norway, which was true. We went to Lillehammar, later made famous by the Winter Olympics in 1994. In the spring I told him that a friend and I had decided to spend the summer traveling through Europe. I'm lucky he didn't give up on me or meet someone else!

I'd met Hella at the Filadelfia church in Stockholm. She was a Finnish refugee, who had grown up in a Christian home in Småland. During the war many children from Finland were sent to Sweden where it was safer. Her last name was Peltola, and we called her "Pelle." We got along really well, so when I began talking of traveling through Europe, she decided to go with me.

I sold my big American car and bought a little Volkswagen Bug that was more economical to drive. We couldn't afford to stay in hotels along the way so we filled my little car with camping equipment, a tent, sleeping bags, and a cook stove. Again I was the only driver; Hella read the map.

We drove through Denmark to Hamburg, Germany where Hella had friends. They had been forced to flee their nice home in Berlin during the war and now lived in a small apartment. Having left everything behind, a beautiful home full of expensive furniture and paintings, they now had other values. Material items had lost their importance; instead they were involved in the church and found much more enjoyment than they ever had in their luxurious dwellings. We went with them to church and experienced a wonderful service.

Germany was struggling with the aftereffects of the war, and in many areas the destruction was still apparent, but they had made amazing progress in rebuilding. We continued down through Stuttgart and Munich, staying at campgrounds along the way. Campgrounds were located on the outskirts of all the major cities and they were well marked. If we missed one anyway, we just continued to the next one. Camping was not expensive, and neither was gas; we cooked our own meals and most of the things we wanted to see were free. We traveled down to Austria, and then continued across through Liechtenstein to Switzerland, three of the most beautiful countries in Europe.

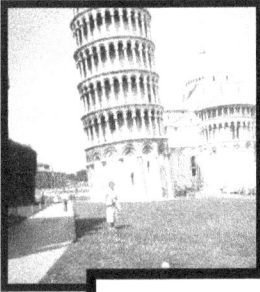

Not having a plan, we went wherever the mood took us. We came to Italy and rode gondolas on the canals of Venice, saw St. Peter's cathedral and the coliseum in Rome, and climbed the 300 steps to the top of the leaning Tower of Pisa. We were camping on one of the islands off the coast of Italy when the weather turned bad. Rain and wind pelted our little tent. The ropes holding our tent shrunk in the rain, pulling the stakes out of the ground, collapsing the tent on top of us. This was our only mishap on the trip, and we considered it just part of the experience.

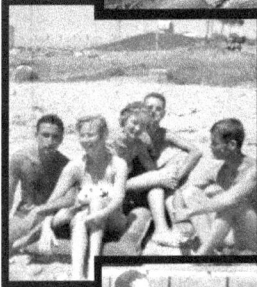

Following the Italian coast north, we came to the Lilliputian country of Monaco, a beautiful place to stop and spend time on the beach, but we never saw the former American actress, Princess Grace. We followed the southern coast of France until we came to Spain. In Barcelona we went to see a bullfight. It was so tense; my knees were shaking when we left. If I never see a bullfight again, it will be too soon.

We decided that we wanted to go all the way to Africa before turning around and heading home. Not wanting to take the car, we parked it on a hill in Gibraltar and walked down to the ferry that went across the strait to Tangier. Hella knew some people who worked at Ibra radio station run by the Swedish Pentecostal church. We were able to visit the station to see how it was run.

We also visited the market, ate couscous and chicken and rode a camel. I had to pay for the camel ride, but it was worth every penny. When we returned after two days in Tangier, we found my little car right where we had left it, unharmed and with everything in it. It must have been the solid rock of Gibraltar!

It was time to head home. We drove north to Portugal. Friends of ours, missionaries in Lisbon, took us around and showed us the city. We visited their church, a fairly large congregation, and had a wonderful time of praise and worship. Language differences fade away when you are praising the Lord. It all becomes a joyful noise.

A girl we knew from Bible school in Stockholm, lived in Madrid. Traveling is so much more fun when you know people along the way. Not only is it fun to be reunited, they can also show you all their favorite places in the city.

There was little to see as we traveled through the French countryside, but Paris was beautiful. We went up to the top of the Eiffel Tower and gazed at the view. We made our way through Belgium and Holland, Germany and Denmark, and were soon back in Sweden. We put a sign on the car that read:

SWEDEN TO AFRICA AND BACK AGAIN!

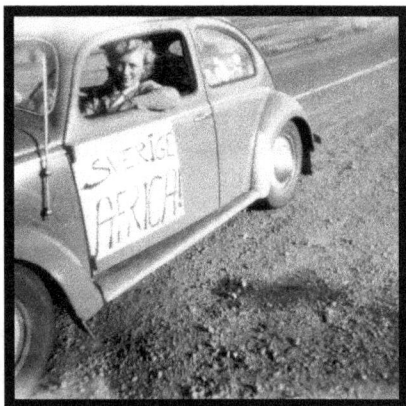

The newspapers came out and interviewed us. It had been a successful trip. All our money was gone, but we had lots of memories instead.

142

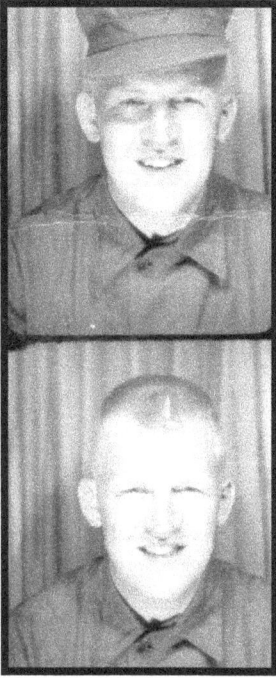

Traveling through Europe I sent a few postcards to Orla, but since he knew that I wasn't home, he didn't write to me. He was always in the back of my mind, and I carried his picture with me. He wrote as soon as he knew I was home again, and sent me pictures he had taken just after enlisting in the army. It was a little shocking. I remember thinking, "Is that what he looked like?"

He asked when I would be coming back. I had been in Sweden for over a year, it was time to go back to America. I booked passage on the Gripsholm, leaving Gothenburg in November 1957.

We stood on the ship that was docked at the so-called "America Dock," and sang the Swedish national anthem. The last line of the song is:

I want to live,
I want to die in the North.

Then we all set sail for America!

Love, Marriage and Babies

Love, Marriage and Babies

We disembarked in New York and I crossed the country by bus. I really wanted to be in Los Angeles, but feared it would be too far from Orla for him to come and visit me. Not wanting to be too blatantly obvious, I decided to settle in San Francisco where I had friends.

Orla came to visit the first week I was back. What had been a small spark erupted into an inferno. It seemed that we had so much in common, both coming from Scandinavia, having grown up on a farm. Although he was not really walking close to the Lord at the time, I rationalized that he was a Lutheran, so he must be o.k. Deep down I knew that it wasn't "quite right," but I was falling in love. He was outgoing, had a great sense of humor, could deliver quick comebacks, and had a marvelous laugh. I think his laugh was one of the things that attracted me from the beginning. They say that the trait that attracts you to someone at first will often be the same thing that irritates you later. Could be some truth in that. I still love his laugh, although sometimes I cringe when I hear him across a crowded room.

Once again it was time to work hard and save money. Passing a restaurant on Montgomery Street I spotted a sign in the window, "Waitress Wanted." I had never worked in a restaurant, never waited tables, but I had cooked and waited on a large family all my life, so when the owner asked if I had any experience I answered that yes, I had a lot of experience. After all, he didn't specify what kind of experience he was looking for. He gave me the job and I soon learned the art of waitressing. I really enjoyed working there, meeting new people and getting to know the "regulars."

At night I worked at a hospital keeping watch over especially difficult, often delusional patients. One night I had a patient who was very frail with I.V.s and monitors hooked to her. Suddenly she was trying to climb out of the bed, saying that she needed to jump out the window. She was old and frail. I was young and strong, but it took all I had to hold her down. I called for help, but it was very scary. I felt an evil presence in the room, an evil spirit trying to kill that woman. I've never felt such an evil power. I would have had a lot of explaining to do if she had been able to get up and get to the window.

I worked three nights a week from 10 pm to 6 am. Sometimes I would come home from the hospital, change clothes and head to the restaurant to work a full shift. Looking back I'm amazed a the tempo I kept, but I was young and strong and used to working hard.

Orla came to see me every weekend. At Christmas I gave him a back scratcher and a book, "The Power of Positive Thinking."

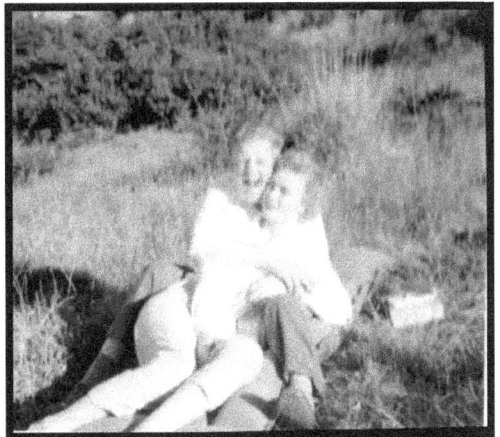

147

In January, he wanted me to come to Sacramento and meet his family. It was about time. Jon and Ragnhild, my best friends in San Francisco, agreed to come along and drive. It was a good thing they did or I may have lost my nerve. After all these years, Ragnhild still teases me about how many times we had to stop at gas stations before we got to 42nd Street.

We met Orla's parents, his younger brother and two younger sisters. They were friendly and kind, but I'm not sure they were thrilled about Orla marrying a Swede.

The house on 42nd Street.

Jens

Orla's father, Jens, lived a fascinating life. Hard working, adventurous and a bit restless, he and his brother left Denmark when they were very young, traveled by boat to Argentina and worked on a cattle ranch for two years before returning to Denmark. They weren't home very long before they were off again seeking adventure, this time in California where they worked on dairy farms. Although he really liked California he decided to go home to Denmark. His brother stayed, met a girl from Denmark, and settled in the Sacramento area.

In Denmark, Jens met Ellen and fell madly in love, but letters from his brother in California fed his desire to return to America. Unable to convince her to come along, he purchased passage on a ship to New York, thinking he could work for a couple of years and come back. Once on board the ship, he missed her so much. Decades later, after they she died, we found letters that he had written to her on this voyage. He had written every day, declaring his undying love. As he neared New York his letters became more regretful. He regretted leaving, regretted spending all that money. When the ship docked in New York, he booked passage on the same ship, returning immediately to Denmark. The rest is history. They married, bought a farm, built a house and had four children.

Life couldn't be more perfect, but Jens continued to dream of going to America. Ellen didn't even want to hear about it, but after listening to him talk about how wonderful it was in the U.S.A. she finally agreed to give it a try. It took them three years to get their immigration papers. They sold their farm, but could only take $50 per family member with them out of the country, the rest had to remain in a bank in Denmark. Flying to New York, they caught a bus across the country to California. Orla was 16 and his youngest sister was only four years old. It was an incredible adventure.

Jens found work easily, first at a dairy farm, later on a gold dredge, and finally, at a creamery that offered insurance for the entire family. They bought a house on 42nd Street, Ellen was working as much as she could. The children were growing and going to school.

Life couldn't be more perfect, but Jens began to have regrets. It had been pretty good back in Denmark, owning his own farm, being his own boss, not working for someone else. This time Ellen wouldn't budge. She had a job, was making her own money and had a certain amount of independence. Besides, she liked America. They stayed and lived on 42nd Street for the rest of their lives.

In 1983 Jens suffered a massive coronary. Doctors performed emergency bypass surgery and he survived but had to take strong medication for the rest of his life. The worst thing, he felt, was that he was no longer allowed to smoke his cigars. Sometimes he would sneak out on the back porch for a couple of puffs. He lived four years after his heart attack, dying peacefully at home on May 24, 1987.

Ellen

Orla's mother, Ellen, was an incredible woman. When they emigrated from Denmark she was 42 years old. Despite her age she learned to speak, read and write English very well. The sound she had trouble with was the "th" sound. Like Viktor Borge always said, "In Denmark we don't stick our tongues out when we talk." She was a woman's libber long before the term was ever coined. All of her children had the same middle name, boy or girl they were all named Just, which was her maiden name. She found work cleaning houses and saved her money in a separate bank account that Jens, her husband, knew little about, and she never told him the balance.

At 55 she decided she wanted to learn how to drive a car. Secretly she began taking lessons, paying for them with her own money. She was always very thrifty, so paying for driving lessons was something she must have considered essential. Passing the written test was no problem, but the driver's test proved to be a challenge. I'm not sure how many times she tried and failed, but she persevered, and, eventually, she passed. They may have just tired of seeing her and gave her a license. She was never a very good driver. Jens knew that once she had gotten her driver's license there would be no stopping her. He figured he might as well help her find a car, so they went out and found a nice Chevy that she paid for herself.

Independent, and now on wheels, she called one day to say that she was coming to visit us in Arcadia. Yes, she would be driving. We worried, but knew that we couldn't stop her. Over the years she made many trips to Arcadia. Not wanting to have traffic on both sides, she would always drive in the fast lane. She was, also, one of the faster drivers on the road. One day she was almost home when she saw the lights of a police car flashing in her rear-view mirror. Instead of pulling over, she continued all the way home, up her driveway and into her carport, the police car following her the whole way. The officer gave her a ticket in her own drive way.

She called Orla the next day and asked, "Can he do that?"

Orla told her she was lucky he didn't charge her with evading arrest!

She was quite a lady, was always kind to me, never cut me down or made me feel I wasn't her first choice for her son. We had a good relationship.

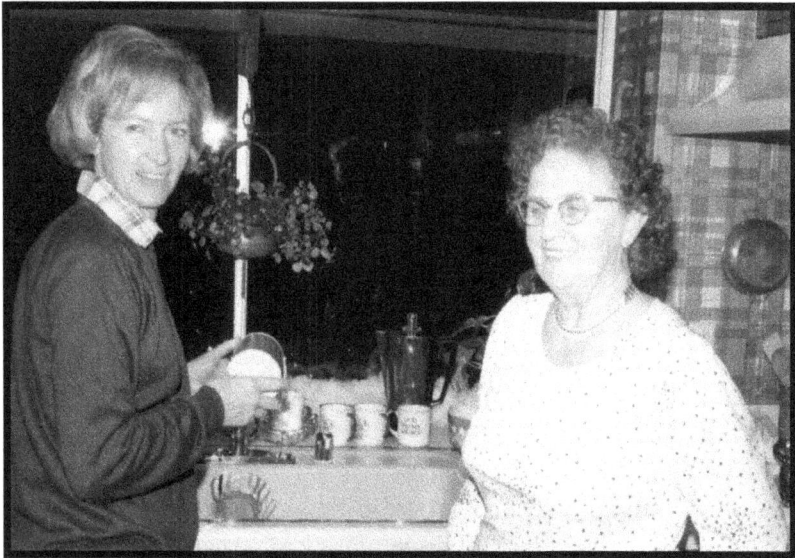

When her husband died she continued to live in her house, traveling often to Denmark and Sweden and to visit us in Los Angeles, and San Diego and then in Colorado. Except for a little high blood pressure she was healthy and independent until she celebrated her ninety-second birthday. Falling ill the day after her party, she was hospitalized and the doctor informed her that, unfortunately her heart, liver and kidneys were giving up. Undaunted she looked up at him and asked, "So how are you going fix that?"

There was, of course, nothing that could be done. When she had stabilized we were able to bring her home. Independent as she was, she insisted on being in her own home. Luckily Orla's sister, Birgitte was able to come to Sacramento and take over her care.

One day, about a month before she died, we were all at the house, sitting in her family room. She turned to Orla and asked him to go to the built in cabinet in the dining room and pull out the bottom drawer. Under the drawer he would find a box that she wanted him to bring to her. It's a good thing she mentioned this because no one would have thought to look there for any valuables! The box in her lap was filled with beautiful Danish silver that she began to sort through, giving something to each of her children. There were five teaspoons that she held in her hands and said, "LaVonne can have these." I'm not sure if she was thinking about LaVonne's five children. It was a very emotional; it was clear that she knew her time was short.

She loved April Fool's Day and would play pranks on everyone in the family. Her final prank was dying on April 1st at 92 years of age.

Jens and Ellen's Golden
Anniversary November 21, 1983

Number 22

On February 22, 1958 Orla proposed and I accepted. We planned a November wedding. We had met on April 22nd, became engaged on February 22nd, and were married on November 22nd. Number 22 has been our lucky number ever since.

We debated over where to live after the wedding. Orla wanted to live in Sacramento, but with temperatures rising to 110 during the summer, I was afraid I wouldn't be able to stand the heat. When he found a job in San Francisco, we agreed to live there.

We were married in the Lutheran Church in Sacramento. Uncle Solomon's son-in-law gave me away. Uncle Solomon, by this time, had died, and his son-in-law was the only male relative I had in California. My sister, Solveig, was my maid of honor and Orla's sisters, Birgitte and Jytte, and two of my friends, Ragnhild and Sandra, were bridesmaids. Orla's brother, Omar, and four of his friends, were groomsmen. I wore a beautiful, white lace, wedding gown, and Orla was dressed in a tuxedo with a white jacket. I have worn that dress every tenth anniversary until now. This year, our 50th anniversary, will be the first major anniversary that I won't be able to wear it; it seems to have shrunk in the closet!

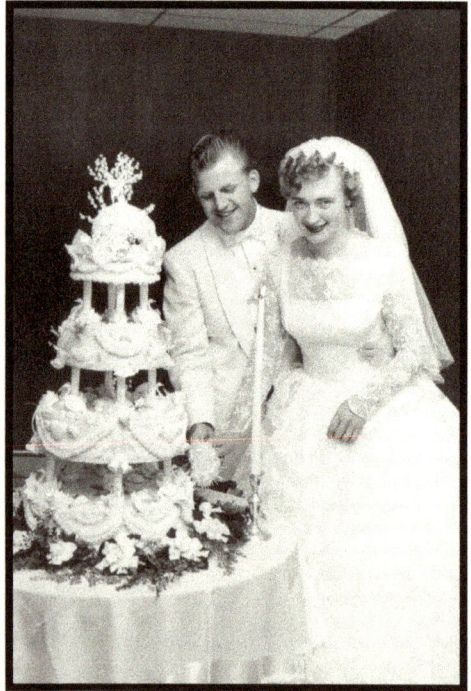

It was a traditional wedding followed by a traditional reception with a four-tiered cake.

❧ 50 Years ❧

1958

1968

1978

1988

1998

2008

Orla's parents celebrated their 25th wedding anniversary the same weekend. When our wedding was over, many of the guests just changed venues and attended their anniversary party. I changed into my "Going Away" dress with veiled hat. We dropped in to their reception and then the two of us went out for dinner.

After the wedding we moved into a small, second floor apartment on Church Street, not far from the Covenant Church. There were about 30 steps leading up to the apartment. Although we had our own bathroom, it was located outside the apartment off a shared corridor. We never knew whom we would meet in the hall on our way to the bathroom. Lilah, a friend who worked at the same restaurant I did, insisted I shouldn't work the first week of my married life. She took vacation from her own shift, worked mine, kept the tips but let me keep the salary. Although I was free for the week, Orla had to look for work. The job offer he had fell through at the last minute and he had to hit the streets. Luckily he found a job within an hour for another painting contractor. We both had jobs we enjoyed and life was good.

Los Angeles

I kept dreaming of, and talking about, Los Angeles, telling Orla how wonderful southern California was, until he agreed to give it a try. We began to make plans. I had customers in the restaurant that came in every day, and, after a while, we got to know each other. I told them that I would be leaving soon; my husband and I were going to Los Angeles. One older gentleman said, "I have a house down there, but since I have a veteran's loan on it I'm not allowed to rent it out. If you want you can live there." I couldn't believe my ears. We sold our furniture, packed our few belongings and headed south. We both felt that an offer of free rent was probably too good to be true, perhaps the place was a dump, but we decided it wouldn't hurt to go there, see the place, and talk to the owners. It was a nice three bedroom house, fully furnished and in a nice area of Monterey Park. I already knew Mr. Moulthrop, and now I got to meet his wife, Jo. Also a very nice person, her grandparents had come from Sweden. We spent a few hours visiting with them and found out they had homes in Hawaii and in San Francisco. They liked us and wanted us to stay in their house. We'd only have to pay utilities. Were we incredibly lucky or incredibly blessed?

It worked out well. We lived there for three years, making it possible for us to save money towards a down payment on a house. A year earlier I had purchased a book titled, "How to Make a Million Dollars in Your Spare Time." Well, that sounded interesting. Reading it, we learned ways to make money through real estate, and wanted to try. Our first property had three rental units. Not having much experience, we went by the book, trying to improve the property. Since we both had other day jobs, we really did do this in our spare time. Orla was working for another painting contractor, and I had a job in an office.

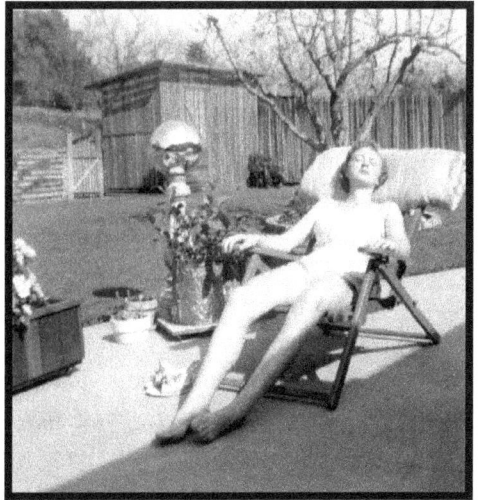

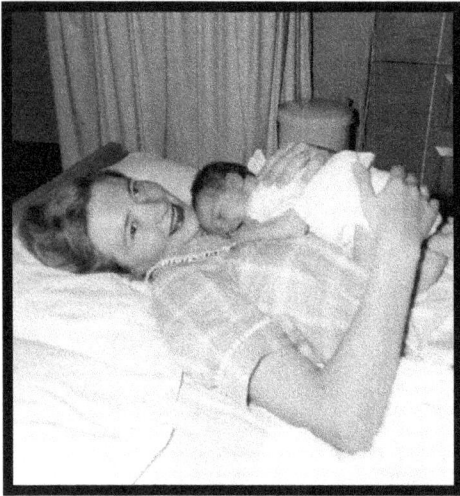

LaVonne

When LaVonne was born in 1961, I quit my office job and became a stay-at-home mom. Like all new parents we thought she was the most beautiful baby, but we were a little surprised that she was a girl. Orla wanted a boy so badly; he couldn't imagine that it could be anything else.

Fathers weren't trusted to behave in the delivery room; they might faint, so he was waiting in the waiting room when the nurse brought our newborn baby out to him. "Here is your little girl, " she said.

A little disappointed he gazed at that wrinkled face and said, "Is that what it is?"

Still a little groggy after a long hard labor, I asked Orla when he came to see me, "Have they circumcised him yet?"

We quickly got over our disappointment, and were thrilled with our little girl. Still living in Monterey Park, in the Mouthrop's house, we brought her home, laid her on the bed and just watched her breathe. She was so tiny and so incredibly perfect.

You knit me together in my mother's womb.
I praise you because I am
fearfully and wonderfully made.
Psalms 139:13-14

Since I was at home, it was natural that I took care of the rentals, and with more time on my hands, I could watch the ads in the newspaper. I spotted an ad with an offer to accept vacant land as a down payment on rental property.

When I first came to California in the early '50's, I wanted to buy some property. A Swedish man we knew was a land agent selling lots in Riverside and Salton Sea. Both, he promised, would be wise investments, appreciating quickly in value. I purchased two lots in Riverside and my friend bought a property in the up and coming Salton Sea Resort. I don't think he was a shyster; I think he truly believed in the future of these properties, but by the early 60's the Salton Sea Resort was a disaster and the two lots I had purchased in Riverside were virtually unmarketable. I called on the ad and they told me they had a property with eleven units available in Downey, and they would take my land as a down payment. We looked at the units and made the deal.

They were four, shabby looking duplexes that needed a lot of work. Now we had fourteen units, but with no money down we were barely breaking even. We did all the fixing up ourselves. Orla taught me how to paint, and as soon as he was off work we would put LaVonne in her infant seat and head up to the apartments to work. When an apartment was finished, painted, cleaned and with new curtains on the windows, we'd sit down and admire our work. One time we sat down, and the wallpaper rolled right off the wall! We just had to get back up and do it again.

A young couple, just arrived from Michigan, rented one of the one-bedroom apartments in Downey. David and Jeanette became very good friends of ours. They helped us show apartments and sometimes baby-sat LaVonne while we were working. One night, when she was about one year old, they bought shrimp for their dinner. When we came to pick her up, they told us that she had eaten most of the shrimp! She has been crazy about shrimp ever since.

Throughout the years they have managed apartments for us in four different locations. We considered them to be two of our dearest friends. Sadly, David is gone now. Jeanette is living in our home in Branson. She is grateful for a place to stay, and we are even more grateful for someone who takes care of our home while we are gone, and who takes care of us when we come to Missouri.

Citizenship

In 1962 I had been living in the United States long enough to be eligible for citizenship. I applied and began studying for the test. To become a citizen I had to know how many states were in the union; what were the three branches of government; how a law comes into being; and something about the history of the United States, like who were the first and sixteenth presidents? I wasn't really sure about all of this, but I did pass and was given a date to appear in court and be sworn in. As a brand new citizen I could choose a brand new name; anything I wanted. I had been christened Maj-Britt Ester Elin. I dropped my third name, feeling that it really wasn't necessary; added an "H" in Esther, to make it more American; and changed the spelling of my first name to May-Britt.

I had always had trouble with my first name. One time at the bank the teller, seeing the unusual spelling, thought I was a major in the army. I have often wished that I had simplified the spelling even more, spelling it MY-BRITT, since that is how it is pronounced in Sweden.

With a new name and a new citizenship I was, and still am, very proud to be an American.

Continuing Education

My father had always maintained that higher education was a waste of time. It would never lead to a better job. Although he realized the importance of being able to read and write, more than that was unnecessary, and six years of schooling was extravagant. It wasn't unusual that he would announce in the morning that he needed help on the farm and we would have to stay home from school. We had no way of notifying our teacher that we wouldn't be coming and we knew he would be cross the next time we did show up at school, but we also knew that we couldn't oppose our father. When we graduated from 6th grade at the age of 13 or 14, we were expected to head out in the world and find work. I had dreams of becoming a nurse, so after working at different jobs for several years I entered nursing school. But my parents' illnesses, and the subsequent death of my mother, made it impossible for me to continue my education. I often wonder what my life would have been like had I been allowed to fulfill my dream.

When I first came to America I found work similar to the jobs I'd had in Sweden. I worked in families, factories and even as a nurse's aide in Chicago. I soon realized that education was highly valued in my new country. In San Francisco, after we were married, I began studying at night school to get my High School Diploma. When we later moved to Los Angeles, I enrolled at East Los Angeles College. I was working days in an office and going to night school. Later we started a business and a family, and I continued to study. Finally, after eight years of studying, I received my Associate of Arts degree!

Although my father was right, my degree didn't give me a better job; it did give me an incredible sense of accomplishment and self-confidence. I still believe in the importance of higher education and often encourage young people to go to college. When our children were growing up I began early to impress on them that they needed to study hard. I never said, "If you go to college." I always said, "When you go to college."

Doolittle

We had been living in Moulthrop's house for three and a half years and felt we were ready to buy a house of our own. We found a small house on Doolittle Avenue, with a huge lot that could be subdivided. In those days there was something called, "build on your own lot." We looked at their models and picked one that would fit on our lot. Living in the front house, we watched our new home being built on the lot behind us. It was exciting to watch it develop. LaVonne was only two years old. Every time I let her go out in the back yard to play she would come back with only one shoe.

Orla Jens

Our new home was ready for us to move into and it was not too soon. I was very pregnant. Orla Jens was born on September 12, 1964. We were so happy when we heard, "It's a boy!"

Our joy was short lived however, when the doctor came into my room the next day and told me there was something very wrong with my baby. I was devastated. He told me they had contacted a specialist who would be coming in to talk to me.

Dr. Farrel came into my room, and was very blunt. I don't know if it would have been easier if she had tried to break the news gently. I was in shock and, perhaps, this was the only way she knew to deliver bad news. She told me that our baby's bilirubin levels were too high, that he would need a blood transfusion. She went on to tell me that levels above 20 could lead to brain damage, and our baby had a level of 28. They gave him three blood transfusions before the bilirubin levels went down. He was out of danger, but we wouldn't know for months, or even years, what damage may have been done. I loved him so dearly. I would have loved him no matter what, but, praise the Lord, he developed normally and had normal intelligence. We tease him sometimes, that if this hadn't happened, he might have been another Einstein, and that might have been unbearable!

For I tell you that their (the children's) angels in heaven always see the face of my Father in heaven.
Matthew 18:10

We named him Orla Jens. There really was nothing to discuss. Orla said, "His name is Orla." Although I like the name Orla, (of course I do) I was afraid that with an unusual name like that he might be teased in school. But, like Zacharias in the New Testament, Orla was adamant.

Raising Children

Our years on Doolittle were among the best years of my life. Having built our home on a back lot, the yard was completely enclosed. We installed a gate at the end of the long driveway, and it was always kept closed. I could, without fear, allow the children outside to play. I have so many fond memories from that place

Happy Playmates

LaVonne was such a compliant child, easy going and happy. She used to put her head on my lap while we were driving. This was long before seat belts and cars seats. We gave no thought to the dangers of children sitting loose in the car. When I was pregnant with Orla Jens she no longer fit between my enlarged stomach and the steering wheel. I told her she would have to wait until the baby came. We had friends at church, Harold and Dottie Allen. When Orla Jens was going to be born, and

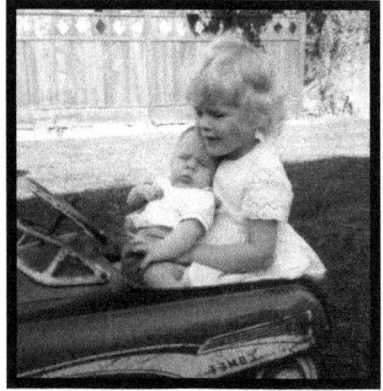

we had to go to the hospital, she said, "I never baby-sit for anyone but I will take LaVonne." I called the next morning to tell LaVonne that she had a baby brother. She responded, "Can I lay in your lap now?"

She played really well with her little brother. They often played that they were running away. Each tying a knapsack to a stick, they would set out on grand adventures in the backyard.

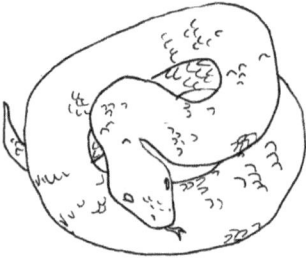

Orla Jens had a rubber snake that was very realistic and very large. He and LaVonne were playing in the kitchen one day. From my office I could hear them babbling on and on. I heard them mention something about making lunch, but didn't think much about it. Later that afternoon we were showing the house to potential buyers. The couple was looking at the kitchen when the wife, who was about eight months pregnant, opened the oven and there was Orla Jens' snake, coiled and ready to strike. She didn't know it was rubber. Screaming and crying, she left the house in a hurry. We lost the sale, but were happy they didn't sue us!

These things happen

Mishaps happen with children around, and with little boys they sometimes happen often.

When we lived on Doolittle, Orla would come home; clean his paintbrushes in the garage; and dumped the paint, thinner and paint cans behind the garage, next to the garbage cans.

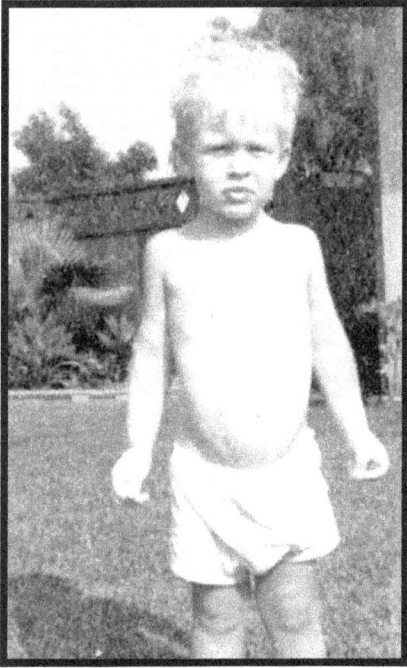

One day Orla Jens was playing in the yard. I went outside to check on him, but couldn't see him anywhere. I finally found him, happily playing among the old paint cans, completely covered in oil paint. He said he was going to paint the playhouse.

I didn't know whether to laugh or cry, so I took a picture. It is my favorite picture of my favorite little boy. Since oil paint doesn't come off easily, I had to scrape off what I could, shave his hair, and wait for the rest to wear off.

Years later, when Orla Jens was a teenager, he and his friend, Harry, went target shooting out in the desert. Using the roof of the El Camino as support, Orla Jens aimed his gun and carefully fired off several shots.

Harry looked at him a bit concerned, "Um, why are you shooting holes in the roof?"

Pale and anxious, he came home that night and had to show his father what had happened.

As usual, when there was a blow up at home, Orla Jens sought solace at the home of his friends, the Dobson's. Shirley met him at the door and asked him how he was doing?

"Not so good, my Dad is mad at me." He answered.

"What did you do, shoot holes in the car?" She asked, intending to make a joke, not realizing how close she was to the truth.

Luckily our son-in-law, Stefan, had grown up in his father's body shop and knew how to fix it. He helped Orla Jens spackle, sand and paint over the holes until the roof was almost as good as new!

167

A woman's prerogative

A woman's closet can be packed full and still she would have nothing to wear. LaVonne was no different. Faced with a closet full of dresses to wear to school, she could not make a decision. Finally I would pick out two to choose from, and the decision came easier. Our friend Jeanette is a tiny little woman with a size two foot. LaVonne was ecstatic the day she realized she could fit Jeanette's shoes. What five year old wouldn't love to wear high heels!

Santa Claus

At Christmas Orla dressed up as Santa Claus, with a very authentic costume that he filled out with a pillow. First he would come to our door surprising LaVonne and Orla Jens. Then he would go to the homes of our friends to surprise their children. Later, when he was in Rotary, he visited orphanages in Mexico, bringing donated gifts to hundreds of orphans. The children also received a Polaroid picture of themselves sitting on Santa's lap. He used his suit so much it eventually wore out, and he had to buy a new one.

One night he went to the home of some friends. The mother in the family had just finished explaining to her children that Santa Claus was not real, when there was a knock on the door. Imagine their surprise when St. Nick was standing outside! As he left he heard one the children exclaim, "See Mom, there really is a Santa Claus!"

Another time one young boy asked him where he had left his reindeer.

"I left them outside." He answered.

When he left, Jon followed him outside to see the reindeer, only to see Santa climbing into a car. Today Jon is a judge in Las Vegas. It's amazing to see what becomes of the children you watched grow up.

One Christmas, when LaVonne was five years old, I decided that it was time she learned to keep a secret. I bought a valet stand for Orla to hang his clothes on in the bedroom, wrapped it up and put it under the tree. I told LaVonne that I had bought a chair for Daddy but she couldn't tell him about it; it was a secret. Despite his pestering her, she never told. Then one night there was a knock at the door. Excitedly the children showed Santa Claus into the house and helped him to a chair. With LaVonne sitting in his lap, Santa eyed the presents under the tree.

"That big present over there," he asked her, "who is that for?"

"That's for my daddy," she answered.

"Well, what's in it?"

Looking Santa Claus straight in the eyes she whispered loudly, "It's a chair!"

Magna Vista

I fell in love with a house on Magna Vista. It really had no street appeal, but it had a wonderful atrium. Surrounded by plate glass windows, with a small pond and a fountain, the atrium was like a beautiful oasis. I just had to have that house. What I didn't know was that those windows were constantly spotty, showing every fingerprint and water spot splashed by the fountain, and that the fish in the pond were always jumping out, flopping around among the rocks and plants. My dream house soon became my nightmare.

169

We were moving from Doolittle to Magna Vista. I was following Orla's truck that was full of furniture and boxes. The children were sitting among all the packing in the back of the truck, Orla Jens holding a shoebox with his pet toad. Suddenly, on El Monte Boulevard, the toad took a giant leap, out of the truck and onto the road. Orla Jens lunged after his pet. Terrified, I watched the scene from my car, afraid that he'd jump out of the truck to catch his toad. Luckily he didn't jump. Devastated, but safe, he arrived at our new home in tears.

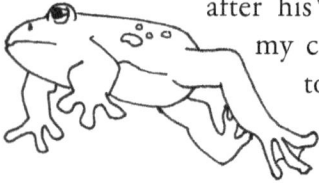

Unfortunately the tears seemed to last on Magna Vista. Although LaVonne quickly made friends with two girls down the street, there didn't seem to be any little boys in the neighborhood. Coming home from her friend's house after playing all afternoon, LaVonne was attacked by the flying fists of a frustrated five-year-old boy. This was so contrary to his usual behavior; I can only guess that he was so jealous he couldn't contain himself.

Accidents and injuries

We bought him a bicycle and he was outside learning to ride. A neighbor came over and asked, "Is that your little boy lying in the street?" He'd lost his balance and had slid across the pavement. You would have thought he had been in a motorcycle accident. He had a huge bump on his forehead and scratches all over his arms, legs and face. He was a real mess.

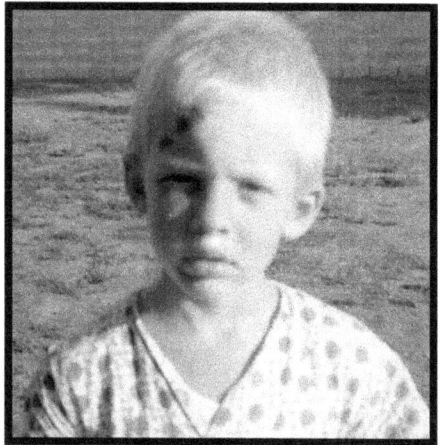

We moved to a house that we'd built on Winnie Way and the children changed schools. Orla Jens was in second grade. The school nurse called me at home; she said he might have a concussion. I picked him up and asked him what had happened.

They had gone out to the playground for recess. Orla Jens was on the swings, swinging higher and higher. "The other kids told me to let go, so I did."

When he was a little older he begged us for a set of weights. Standing in the family room holding the barbells above his head, he fell backwards. The weights came crashing down, breaking his arm on impact. It was a while before he tried lifting weights again.

School

Living on Doolittle the kids rode the school bus to school every day. After watching LaVonne board the bus every morning for three years, Orla Jens was anxiously waiting for his turn. He was so excited to start kindergarten and ride the bus and absolutely did not want me to take him to school or even pick him up at the bus stop that was only a couple houses from our home. One day he came home really late from the bus stop. I asked him where he had been. "Oh," he replied nonchalantly, "I took a short-cut."

When LaVonne was only four years old she memorized an entire book that she would "read" to visitors. Although I knew she wasn't really reading, it did impress our guests. When she started school she learned quickly, recognizing whole words on sight. Her first grade teacher said, "She's college material."

Questions Children Ask

Orla Jens, on the other hand, had difficulties learning to read. I took him to Arcadia Reading Clinic on Baldwin Avenue. They recommended he read to me every morning, and we decided he would read a chapter from the bible. One morning he was reading Matthew chapter five, when he came to the verse

And if your right hand causes you to sin,
cut it off and throw it away.
Matthew 5:30

"Mom," he asked, "What does that mean?"
I launched into a rather long-winded explanation of the scripture. Quickly disinterested he interrupted me, "Ah, it doesn't matter. I'm left-handed anyway!"

Although his early academic accomplishments were slow in coming, he later graduated from college magna cum laude. Today he reads and interprets my legal papers, earning the honorary title of "attorney," at least in our house.

When the children were young we went camping by a lake with another family. Standing on the rocks fishing, LaVonne noticed a "No Swimming" sign. Puzzled, she asked, "What happens if we fall in?"

Message Wall

On Winnie Way, in the office, we had a bare white wall and nothing to hang on it. I decided to let the children write and draw anything they wanted on it, as long as they gave their contribution careful thought. They were old enough, so I knew they understood that this was not something you could do anywhere else. We filled that wall with scripture, poems, wise quotes and drawings and it became a wonderful focal point, capturing the attention of everyone who came to visit.

Pets

Over the years we had a menagerie of animals.

A tortoise that Orla found in the desert, brought home, painted our address on its shell, and let go in the back yard. It was a wanderer, taking off on walkabouts until a neighbor would spot it and carry it back to our house.

Two bunnies, Peter and Polly, later released at the County Sheriff's shooting range, a big wilderness where we hoped they would live a long and productive life.

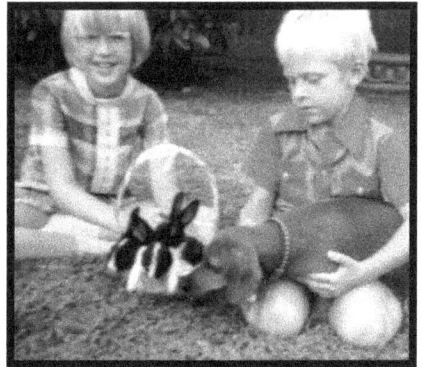

We celebrated Midsummer with hundreds of other Swedes at Vasa park in Los Angeles. The children called it the "frog park" because the place was crawling with frogs. Every year they would fill coffee cans full of frogs, bring them home and release them in the yard. That could be where Orla Jens' toad came from.

Flicka, the dachshund, became Orla Jens' dedicated antagonist. He was only three years old when we brought home this tiny puppy. Orla Jens would tease her and pull her ears and tail and she would chase after him and nip at his heels. The first time she came into heat I put up a plywood board to keep her in the dinette area. Someone came to the door and Orla Jens ran to answer. "Come on in," he said, "but be careful. The dog is overheated."

Their love-hate relationship continued throughout the years. On Winnie Way he was older but still teasing her mercilessly. Still, she insisted on sleeping in his bed. One night we heard the customary growling and barking mixed with a child's laughter that suddenly changed to shrieks of pain. Rushing in to see what had happened I found Orla Jens lying on his back, one eye covered in blood. Flicka had bit him on the cheek, narrowly missing his eye. The dog was obviously feeling terrible remorse, but we knew that Orla Jens was equally to blame, so we didn't punish her.

On Magna Vista, we had a big yard. I built a shed in the corner and got a sheep from a farmer. What I'd envisioned as a "Mary's little lamb" turned out to be a big, ugly ram that wanted nothing to do with us.

A friend of ours gave us a couple of ducks. We had a plastic wading pool for them to swim in, but they were partial to the patio outside our master bedroom, and would crap all over the place. When we tired of this we drove them back to our friends house in the middle of the night and threw them over the fence into his yard. Finding them the next morning, he called to tell us the ducks had flown home. We told him that it was o.k.; they were better off there anyway.

We had rabbits. First we had one. Then, wanting the kids to experience the rabbits having babies, we searched for a female. It isn't easy to tell the sex of a rabbit. Before we knew it we had six rabbits, all males. Finally, we borrowed the neighbor's female, and she had five bunnies, which eventually escaped and took off all over the neighborhood.

We hatched eggs in a small incubator and had chickens. When they got big we drove them over to our friend's house, the same friend who had the ducks, and dumped them in his yard.

Every time the kids went to a school carnival, they would bring home goldfish in a plastic bag, goldfish that, if they survived the first day, never seemed to die. I remember having to change that dirty bowl every couple of days, hoping that one morning, I would come out and find that fish floating belly up.

We had a never-ending series of assorted hamsters, mice, lizards and snakes.

We had cats that had kittens, and dogs that had puppies; even one of the hamsters had babies the day after we bought her. She ended up eating all of them.

Orla Jens had a rat that sat on his shoulder when he did his homework, and a bird that he could never teach to talk.

LaVonne bought a Pug dog, that got sick and cost us hundreds of dollars in Veterinary bills, but we didn't want her to suffer the despair of watching her pet die. Percy loved to ride a bike. Wrapping her hind legs around the crossbar and hanging onto the handlebars, she turned her face toward the wind and smiled. Orla Jens won a contest at school for the "Best Decorated" bike, decorated with a live dog.

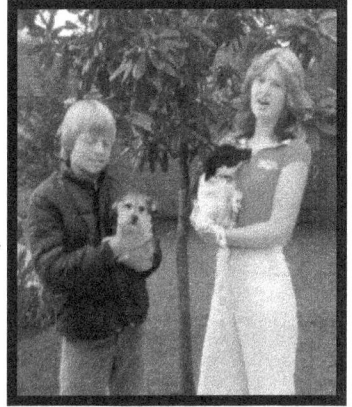

On Winnie Way we bought two puppies from a pet shop. I called them Double Trouble, because they were impossible to housebreak. After them, I vowed I would never have a dog again.

But Orla Jens desperately wanted another dog, and was constantly saying, "If we only had a dog." Feeling sorry for him, but not willing to take on another puppy, I prayed to the Lord, asking Him to find us a dog that was already housebroken.

A friend of ours had a taken in a stray dog that had been roaming her neighborhood. She was such a pretty little dog, with a red coat and a curly tail. I brought her home in our brand new Buick and she threw up all over the front seat. I hadn't asked Orla, so we smuggled her in and hid her in the pool house. The next morning, after carefully breaking the news to Orla, we went out to the pool house so he could meet our new addition. Opening the door we were enthusiastically greeted by a small dog, tail wagging and barking among shards of destruction. She had destroyed the door and the carpet, and both had to be replaced. Uncharacteristically Orla kept his cool, and despite everything, we kept her.

She was a wonderful dog. She loved to chase balls and Frisbees into the pool. If no one would throw them for her she would drop them in herself and jump in after. We had to hide the toys in the winter when it was too cold for her to be swimming.

When she died, we missed her terribly, and though I sometimes wish we had a dog, I don't think we could ever find another Shatzie.

LaVonne

LaVonne Esther
Born July 28, 1961

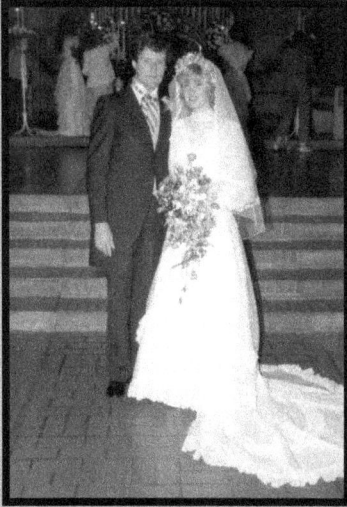

Wed Stefan Quinth
June 19, 1982

LaVonne lives in Sweden with her family. She and her husband own a production company, producing documentaries from around the world. Pictured here with their five children. From left to right: Nicolas, Stefan, Stephanie, Erik, LaVonne, Oliver, Jonathan.

Orla Jens

Orla Jens
Born September 12, 1964

Wed Darla Williams
November 29, 1991

*Orla Jens lives in Colorado Springs. He and Darla own a
construction company, Orla Homes, continuing the tradition
of building quality custom homes. Pictured here with their two
daughters. From left to right: Lydia, Jens, Darla, Mallory*

Bonus Children

Besides our own children there have been several others who have come into our lives for shorter or longer periods of time, many became very dear to us.

Jon and Jennifer

As newlyweds we lived in an apartment right behind the Covenant Church in San Francisco. When we moved to Los Angeles we began attending the Covenant Church in Pasadena. We were in a Sunday School class for young married couples, a fun and social group where we made many life long friends. Many of the couples started their families about the same time that we did, and so our children were all around the same age.

Ken and Carol Norheim became very good friends of ours. They had two children; Jon, who was a year younger than LaVonne; and Jennifer, who was a year older than Orla Jens. In the early '70's Ken became ill with a rare disease, Granuloma. Carol, a college professor at Pasadena City College, struggled to care for him and her children while trying to make ends meet and cover hospital costs. Hers is a story of faith, perseverance, and the Grace of God in times of trouble. Ken fought his disease, many times coming close to death. He saw specialists all over the country. When Ken and Carol were both away consulting specialists, we took care of Jon and Jennifer. One summer Ken wanted to visit his relatives. Orla, who had his pilot's license at the time, rented a small plane and flew him to North Dakota.

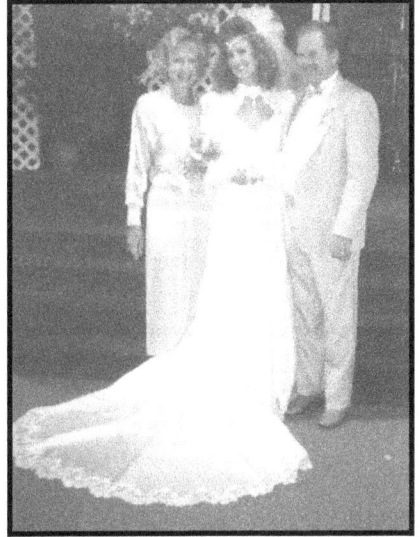

Ken lost his battle in 1983, having lived long enough to see both of his children reach adulthood. Jon is now a judge in Los Vegas. Jennifer came to live with us for two years while she attended Pasadena City College. She later became a Marriage and Family Therapist. When she was planning her wedding she asked Orla to walk her down the aisle, something he considered a great honor.

"Mary" – a Young Mother

When our children were pre-teens we had the opportunity to help a young pregnant girl by offering her a place to stay during the last months before her baby was born. "Mary" – not her real name – was a lovely girl and fit in well with our family. She was open about her circumstances and her choice to give birth to her child rather than have an abortion. Her baby was born on New Year's Day. Wanting her baby to have more than she felt she could offer she chose to give it up for adoption, never even seeing the face of her son. Her cheerful spirit and the openness in which she shared her mistakes and her choices, was a good influence on our children and a blessing to our family.

João (John)

When LaVonne moved to San Diego to go to Point Loma College, we volunteered to host a Rotary exchange student from Brazil. João lived with us for six months, went to high school with Orla Jens, and went with us on our summer vacation. He became like a son, and it was hard to say good-bye when it was time for him to go home.

Three years later he came back for college. Living with us, he bicycled around town, picking up odd jobs and getting to his classes. He really impressed us with his determination. After returning to Brazil he finished school, and got a job for a Brazilian bank that eventually sent him to New York, where he now lives. He still stays in touch, and still calls us "Mom and Dad."

I recently received a letter from John.

Hi Mom,

I cannot say enough of how important you, Dad, LaVonne and Orla Jens have been to me with your love and support. I still look at the time when you guys took me as an exchange student in 1980 as the best, happiest time in my life.

Love,
João

Ingela

When Orla started the project in San Marcos we bought a house on Mulberry Street across from the building site. Orla converted the garage into an office, and lived in the house. Sometimes I came down for a week or a weekend, and sometimes Orla came home to Arcadia. Orla was becoming more involved with the community in San Marcos. He served as president of the Rotary club and later as president of the Chamber of Commerce. Tired of commuting back and forth we sold the house in Arcadia, bought a house in Carlsbad on Alicante Road and totally remodeled it. Although I had thought that I would never want to leave Arcadia, I did enjoy living in Carlsbad. We had a view of the ocean; the flowers were beautiful; and we were away from the smog.

One night, while we were still on Mulberry, I had a dream. The phone was ringing and someone answered it and said, "It's for you. It's from heaven. It's an old pastor from Sweden."

It was Pastor Lewi Petrus; he told me, "The Lord has a message for you. He is going to give you a burden."

I asked, "What kind of burden?"

"A burden for young people," he answered.

Then I woke up, but the dream that had seemed so real, stayed with me.

Not long after that my niece called from Montana. We talked about her coming to California for a while. She was 18 years old, and I thought I could help her go to college. What I didn't know was that she had dropped out of school when she was 16, run away from home, and now had problems. It was a challenge to have Ingela move in with us. Her lifestyle and habits didn't really fit ours, but I loved her deeply and the Lord gave me a burden for her. I walked the streets at night, crying out to Him to save her. Ingela had no trouble finding jobs, often coming home announcing that she had a new job or an extra job. She moved out with a friend for a while, and then moved back in with us. There were bouts with drinking that would terrify us. We spoke to her of the Lord and His salvation, but didn't press. We just continued to pray and pray for her.

Then one day, when she had been living with us for a year or so, she sat down and prayed with us. Although she had given her heart to Jesus when she was 14, and was baptized, she had since then fallen away. Now she turned back to Him, asking forgiveness and help to get away from her problems. That just goes to show that the Lord never lets go.

Ingela became a new person. She went back to school, getting her G.E.D. and continuing with college. She found a job with an insurance company, beginning at the bottom and rising quickly to a very high position with her own office.

She met David, a young Christian man aspiring to become a police officer. We helped her plan her wedding in the little chapel on Mulberry. Orla had the honor of walking her down the aisle.

Today they live in Escondido and have four children. David serves on the Escondido Police Force.

We have been so blessed by this. Not only has the Lord allowed us to be a small part in His great plan for Ingela, He has also given us another child. Ingela has become like a daughter to us, filling a space in our hearts we hadn't realized was empty.

"For I know the plans I have for you," declares the Lord, "plans to prosper you and not to harm you, plans to give you hope and a future. Then you will call upon me and come and pray to me, and I will listen to you. Jeremiah 29:11-12

Grandparents

We have seven grandchildren; LaVonne has four boys and a girl and Orla Jens has two daughters. Orla Jens lives nearby so we get to see the girls often. LaVonne comes from Sweden and stays for a couple of intense months. They say that grandchildren are life's dessert. I love having them in the house, enjoying their sweetness and their exuberance, and then, when I am tired, I turn them over to their parents.

In addition to our "real" grandchildren, we have several "bonus" grandchildren. Although they don't call us Grandma and Grandpa, Ingela's four children are very dear to us. And then we have the Cornuke twins.

When we moved to Colorado we built a house on Star Ranch Road. Bob and Teresa Cornuke built a house just below us. They were wonderful neighbors and we soon became close friends. Despite our age difference, Teresa and I connected right away. One day we were sitting around the table at our house when Bob mentioned that life with Teresa was never dull. "It's like living with Lucille Ball," he said.

"What does that make me then," I asked, "Ethel?"

From then on we were known as Lucy and Ethel.

Bob and Teresa longed for a child but found that pregnancy would have to be achieved through in vitro fertilization. We promised that, when they were ready, we would drive them to the hospital. They set up an appointment with their doctor at the Swedish Hospital in Denver.

The procedure was successful and Teresa was expecting twins. We teased them that we were present for the conception! In February 1998, Teresa gave birth to a little boy and a little girl. I was so honored when she asked me to be present in the delivery room and witness their birth.

Connor and Shannon are now eleven years old, and they are very special to me. To them we are "Grandma and Grandpa" What honorable titles! We feel so blessed to be part of this special family.

Making Money

Making $$

Our career in real estate began when I read the book, "How to Make a Million Dollars in Your Spare Time." We literally began in our spare time, buying property and fixing it up when Orla came home after a days work with a painting contractor. By the time we moved to Doolittle, we had eleven units and Orla had his own painting business.

Fred Shubin, who had sold us the property in Downey, saw that we had done well with what we had, and asked if we were interested in buying some more units. He had ten units right next to the freeway in East Los Angeles. They were fairly new, which was a step up for us, and he was willing to sell them for nothing down. I planted a palm tree in the courtyard of those buildings. Forty years later we drove by to take a look. The palm tree was still there, towering above the rooftops.

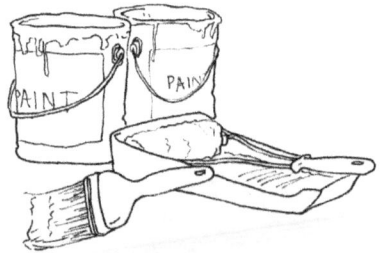

We purchased eighteen units in Baldwin Park and five units on Marengo Street in East Los Angeles. These were in marginal areas, which meant lots of work. One of the tenants in Baldwin Park had a lot of pets. She kept an alligator in the tub. When we told her that was not allowed, she exclaimed, "What else would I use a tub for?"

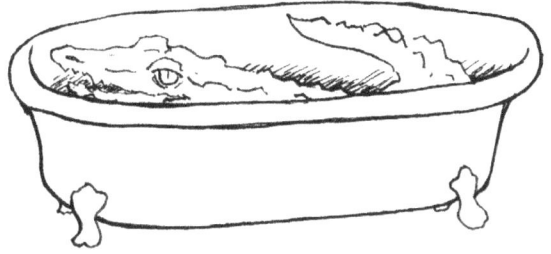

We bought a two story, four-unit building in Los Angeles. It was so old the curb still had the rings they used to tie their horses. There were times we wished we didn't have them. The health department contacted me to tell me there was a problem with the building. I wasn't aware of any problems, so I arranged a meeting with them. They showed me a big hole in the ceiling of one of the apartments. It hadn't been there before, so I asked the tenant when and how that hole came about.

He told me, "I made the hole to let the smog out."

"But that wouldn't let the smog out," I argued.

"Sure does," he countered, "I threw some flour up and it sucked it right out."

How do you argue with that?

One of the worst properties we owned were two small houses in Monrovia. They were single wall construction; if you nailed something on the inside of the wall it came out on the outside.

Most of these properties were not large enough to warrant a manager, and I would have go and collect the rents myself. I didn't particularly like that aspect of the job; the tenants, if they were even home, were not always thrilled to see me. I often had to make several trips each month. Otherwise I found the work very stimulating, especially when I could solve a problem or fix something a man had not been able to do.

We had ten units in Pasadena, a nice building with underground parking. The Fire Department was constantly after us to keep a big water hose or a fire hydrant in the parking area. Although we tried both the hose and the hydrant, it was impossible. They were stolen as soon as we hung them up. We did have a manager there, but he was not very effective. When he couldn't collect the rent I would have to go myself. One tenant told me that she didn't have the rent money, but if I came back on Wednesday she would give it to me. Unfortunately, I was detained on Wednesday and couldn't come until Thursday. When I knocked on her door she told me, "You didn't show up yesterday. Now I've already spent that money!"

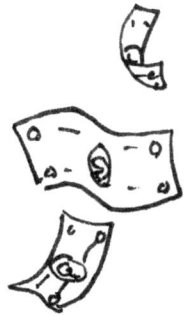

One night the manager called at two o'clock in the morning. "I'm calling because they are making so much noise next door. If I can't sleep then you don't get to sleep either!"

It could be very frustrating sometimes.

We had four units in Monrovia. When we bought the property there was one tenant that owned 20 guinea pigs. In his backyard there was a pond covered in a thick layer of algae.

190

I needed a permit from the city and an inspector came out and we were talking in the backyard. Thinking the pond was a concrete patio, and it really did look like one, he stepped onto it and sank down into the water. He was so embarrassed, and so was I, but I got my permit.

Arcadia

Early on we bought a property on Duarte Road with a small house in front and ten units in the back. David and Jeanette lived in the house and managed the apartments. I loved having apartment buildings in Arcadia. One day a realtor called and solicited a property on Arcadia Avenue. It wasn't even listed yet, but they thought that given an offer, the owners might sell. I was so excited, we went right up to Arcadia Avenue and looked at it, liked it, and placed an offer. It was accepted and we bought the property.

Another property on Arcadia Avenue became available and we bought that one too.

Once, when Orla was out of the country, a property on Fairview Avenue went up for sale. I looked at it, liked what I saw, and placed an offer subject to Orla's approval. When he returned he liked it too, approved my offer and the property was ours.

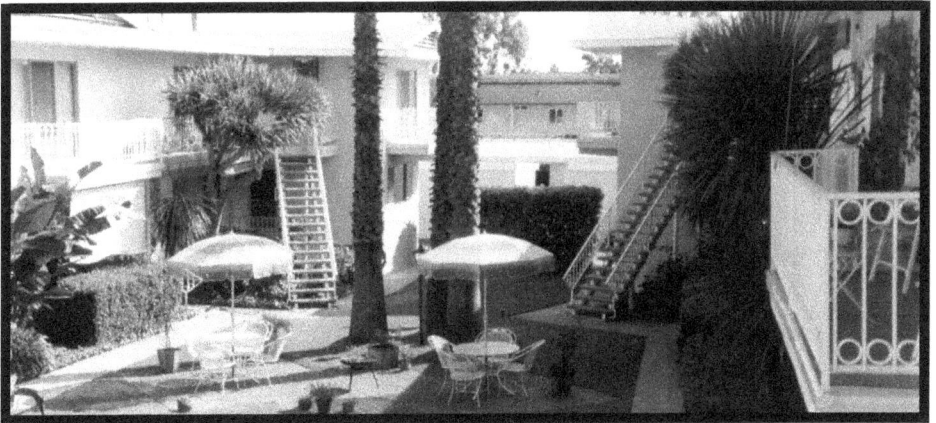

Big Bear

I was always scouring the ads looking for interesting properties. One day I saw an ad for a mobile home park in Big Bear. We decided to drive up there and take a look. It had 75 spaces, a nice three-bedroom house in the middle and a recreation hall. We didn't know the first thing about running a mobile home park, but figured that we could learn. The numbers made sense. They were asking for $80,000 down and had four low-interest loans. We didn't have the down payment, but were able to borrow from the bank, so we made an offer and it was accepted. With five loans, it was pretty tough in the beginning, but we were able to pay off several of those loans fairly quickly.

The house in the middle of the park was also the office. In the beginning we had to go up there as often as we could

to learn the business, but we turned that time into a vacation get-away-for the family. We learned to ski, something we have all enjoyed.

The property came with a 1939 dump truck and an old golf cart. LaVonne had a Teen Slumber party up there, writing in the invitation, "no drugs and no alcohol," to calm any suspicious parents. It was a lot of fun. Orla gave everyone a ride in the back of the dump truck. We received several thank you notes from parents whose kids had had a nice time.

We converted one of the buildings on the property into a cabin, furnishing it with used furniture. I was able to stock the kitchen with our old china and silverware I had bought at a garage sale. One weekend Solveig came with us and stayed in the new cabin. She was doing the dishes and wiping the silverware when she asked me, "Why do you have sterling silver up here?" I was surprised; I had only paid $2 for the silverware. I didn't know it was sterling silver! I took it with me to a department store and traded it in for $90 worth of silver that matched my set at home. Since then I've been hooked on garage sales. You never know when you'll make a superb deal!

We hired managers for the park, and they lived in the big house with the office. We used the smaller cabin when we came up for weekends; otherwise we rented it out to tourists. The mobile home park turned out to be a lot of work, but it was also a lot of fun.

Evictions

Evicting people is never any fun, but it is something that has to be done. Fortunately we never had to evict any families with small children. There is one eviction however, that stands out in my mind as rather comical.

We bought a strip mall in San Marcos thinking that managing a shopping center would be easier than apartments. We were wrong. California was in the middle of a recession. Attracting businesses, and getting them to stay took all the creativity and stamina I could muster. No sooner would I fill a storefront then another business would give notice. A strip mall with too many vacancies will soon be completely empty. I had to keep filling those spaces.

Although I offered many incentives, like the first six months free, I did expect to eventually begin collecting rent. There was a restaurant that had been in the center for ten years when they changed ownership. The new owner didn't think paying rent was a priority. We served them with an eviction notice for non-payment of rent, but I don't think they took it seriously. When we called the Marshall, who would perform the physical eviction, he suggested we do it right in the middle of the lunch hour. "It'll be more fun that way," he said.

We all arrived at the restaurant at noon, the Marshall going in to inform everyone in the place that this restaurant was being closed down. Anyone still eating would be allowed to stay and finished their meal; everyone else was asked to leave. The owners were given a short amount of time to gather any personal items while the Marshall waited. Then, when everyone had cleared the premises, he locked the doors. It was actually pretty funny to watch.

I'll include another story from the shopping center. This is Orla's favorite story; he loves to tell it. I don't, but this one's for you, Honey!

I had a problem with the heating unit on the roof, so I asked Orla to come down and take a look at it. He brought his ladder and climbed up on the roof. One of the store owners came out and asked him what he was doing. Orla answered, "I'm just checking something on the roof."

"Oh," said the man, "you must be the son of that woman who runs this place."

Orla got a big kick out of that, and didn't bother to relieve the man of his disillusionment.

Lawsuit

We owned a store building in Monrovia that we rented to a furniture retailer. They signed a ten-year lease and seemed like nice people. We thought it was a pretty good deal. We made some improvements on the property including replacing the roof. Five or six years later we had a terrible rainstorm. They called to tell us the store was completely flooded and the roof was leaking terribly. It seemed very strange. Why would a brand new roof leak? Orla went over to check it out. The store owner met him at the door, crying his heart out, saying, "I'm ruined! I'm ruined! I've lost everything!"

Inside, the store was completely flooded, the furniture was soaked and the ceiling was dripping. Bewildered, Orla went out to the truck, got his ladder and was climbing up to the attic. Now the store owner got nervous. "You don't need to go up there," he stuttered. "That isn't necessary. I have insurance that will cover the damages."

But Orla wouldn't be stopped; he had to find out what was going on. Climbing up the ladder he saw that the attic was bone dry! No wonder the store owner was nervous! He had flooded his store with a water hose. We understood that he planned to collect on our insurance. It takes all kinds. It has surely been an interesting business.

Orla's Construction

It sounds like I did most of the work, but that's not true. In the very beginning we worked together fixing up apartments. When we built our house on Doolittle we used a "build on your own lot" company. They did all the work. A while later we had a couple of lots that we wanted to build on. Once again we used the "build on your own lot" company, but this time we thought there were certain aspects of the building we could do ourselves, like putting in the driveway and things like that. That's how it started. Before long, Orla had his contractor's license and had started Orla's Construction. At first he built one or two houses. Then he built five at a time. In Arcadia he developed eleven houses and had to put in the street and all the underground sewers. His biggest project was in San Marcos where he did a subdivision with 200 houses.

But this story is about me. I'll let him reveal his own secrets.

197

Colorado Springs

The 1980's recession finally reached California just as we were finishing up the project in San Marcos. Again, the Lord was with us. Real estate sales dropped to a new low, nothing was selling, but we had sold nearly all of the houses we had built; only eight remained. Those we rented for many years before they could finally be sold.

By the time the recession hit California, other parts of the country were already recovering. Orla Jens, in Colorado Springs on a working vacation, looked at some lots. Coming home, he suggested we should buy some property and start building in Colorado. Orla and Orla Jens flew up and purchased a number of lots. They also bought a small house where they could live while they were building. Again I commuted, this time from Carlsbad to Colorado, coming to visit for a week or a weekend.

Never, in all my wildest dreams, did I ever think we would leave California permanently. Colorado was just a temporary project until the economy out west picked up. But we liked it up there in the mountains. Orla Jens and his wife, Darla, decided that they wanted to live in Colorado. A lot of our friends from California had moved to Colorado Springs, so we already knew some people and we made new friends. My nephew, Dwight, and his family also lived there. We built a house for ourselves on Star Ranch Road. I continued to commute to California, taking care of business and the apartment buildings. When we finally decided to sell the house on Alicante, we bought a mobile home in San Marcos. It was so hard to leave a place where I had lived for so many years, much harder than it had been to leave Sweden.

Orla and Orla Jens continued to work together, building custom homes and commercial buildings, until Orla retired in 1999. We built a new home farther up the hill inside a gated community, where we now live. Orla Jens and Darla live nearby.

I have thoroughly enjoyed working and it was very hard for me to retire. I did it in stages, selling off one property at a time until all I had left was Duarte Road and Arcadia Avenue. They are also sold now, and I am fully retired and thoroughly enjoying that too.

Orla J. Pedersen, Retired
May-Britt Pedersen, Retired
No Houses for Sale; No Apartments for Rent

Colorado Srpings, CO

Branson, MO

Looking Back

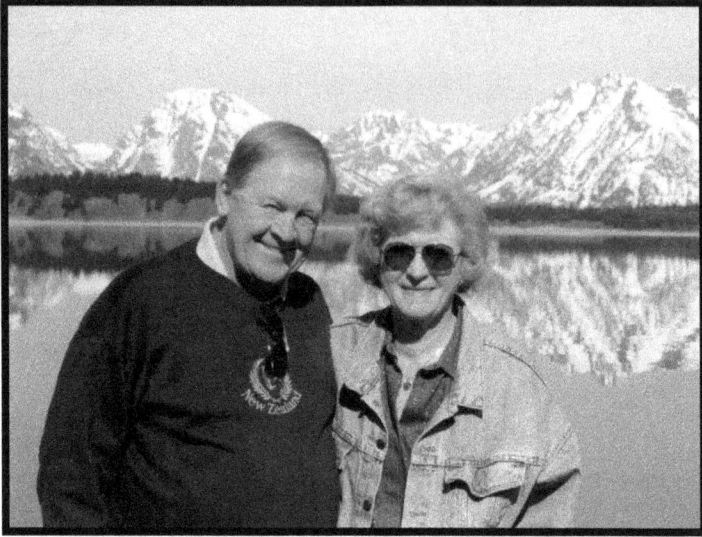

Places I've been

We have been privileged to travel to many countries over the years. At first we made trips to Europe and of course we went home to Sweden and Denmark.

In 1971, we took the children to Sweden for Christmas. It was the first time we took them abroad and they were excited about everything, especially the airplane. It was wonderful to be home for Christmas. My father was still alive and we celebrated at his house in Klerebo. When we came home the neighbor lady asked Orla Jens what he liked the most in Sweden.

He answered, "The Swedish pancakes!"

In 1973 we went to Denmark with Orla's parents. We showed the children the farm where Orla grew up, visited relatives with farms and animals, and took them to Legoland. At one farm someone let the pigs out, and we chased them all over the farm before we rounded them up and got them back to their pen.

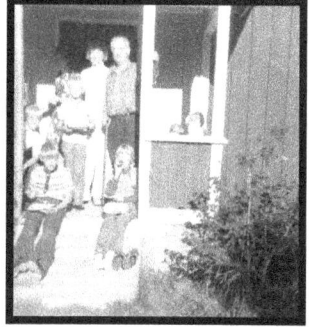

We visited Sweden about every other summer. I think it is so good for children to travel, they learn and experience so much. There is a certain risk involved though, LaVonne met and married a Swedish man, and now lives in Sweden. They travel extensively, taking their five children with them whenever they can.

For our 15th wedding anniversary we took the family to Mexico. We climbed the Aztec pyramids, visited the silver mines in Taxco, and water-skied in Acapulco.

Of course we also traveled in the United States. We visited relatives in Illinois, Florida, Oregon, and Montana. One summer we took four teenagers, our two plus our exchange student, João, and his friend, Jill, on a trip to Arizona in a motor home. We hiked the Grand Canyon, rented a houseboat on Lake Powel, and saw London Bridge at Lake Havasu.

As empty-nesters we have traveled to many exciting places in the world. We've made frequent visits to Sweden, visiting LaVonne and her family, as well as my siblings.

We've revisited Mexico many times, both on our own and with Rotary. Orla's Rotary club in Arcadia helped several orphanages south of the border, and he was very much involved in the Christmas trips, as well as supervising various building projects.

We traveled to India with our friends, Sam and Adela Kameleson. It was so interesting to see India together with people who really know the country. From there we went to Sri Lanka, such a beautiful island country. We fell in love with a young girl, almost bringing her home to live with us, but it was too difficult to make the arrangements. Like most things, it probably wasn't meant to be.

We visited missionary friends in Austria, and went with them into northern Italy.

In December 1997, LaVonne gave birth to her youngest child, Oliver. It was a difficult delivery and she nearly died. We were just leaving on a trip to Australia and New Zealand. We kept in touch by phone from Auckland, Sydney, and Melborne. It was a wonderful trip to beautiful places, marred only by our concern for our daughter. At some point on our trip LaVonne mentioned that her husband, Stefan, had to leave on business and she would be alone with the children. She was much too weak to care for them by herself, and wondered if I could come for a month to help her. This was one of the only times Orla encouraged me to go. He never liked being left at home, but this time he said, "You'd better go."

I left the day after we returned from Australia. As LaVonne regained her strength, I cared for the children, sending the older ones off to school and packing the smaller ones off to day-care. It was heavy work, but I was thankful that I could be there to help LaVonne and to spend time with my grandchildren. Seeing Oliver when he was so small was also a special time.

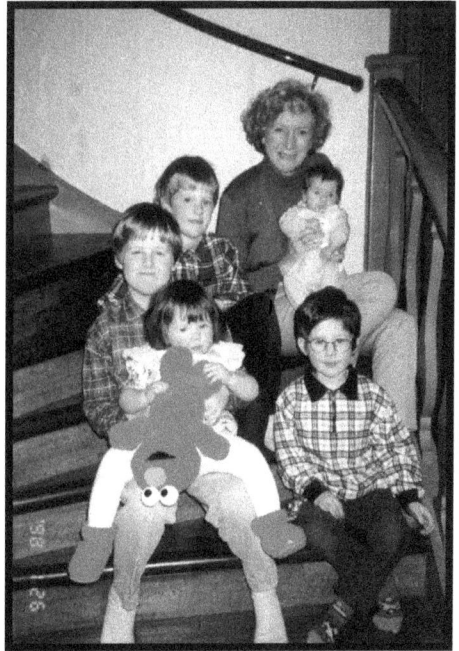

From the top: Me holding month-old Oliver, Erik, Jonathan with Stephanie in his lap, and Nicolas.

205

Our most memorable trip was to Israel with Dr. Roy Blizzard. Of all the places we have visited this is the only place where I would like to return. Walking the same roads as our Lord, sitting on the hillsides, seeing the Jordan River, Jerusalem and the Garden Tomb, Dr. Blizzard made it all come to life. It was an incredible experience. We even took part in an archeological dig!

In 2004 our daughter LaVonne and her husband, Stefan were planning a road trip up the Alaska Highway. They had made the same trip with their five children in 2001, staying on Kodiak for two months before flying home to Sweden. Now they asked if we would join them on this exciting road trip. Overwhelmed at first, we quickly warmed to the idea and began looking at motor homes in which to make the journey. LaVonne and her family left Colorado in their van a few days before we did. They wanted to stop in southern California and spend a week at Disneyland. We decided to meet them in Santa Rosa and continue from there. We drove through the big redwood forest in northern California. I had not been there in many years. When we had been driving for a week, we finally made it to Dawson Creek and the beginning of the Alaska Highway! Imagine driving for a week to get to the beginning of the road! Six days later we boarded a ferry that took us to Kodiak. After ten days on beautiful, wet Kodiak, we flew home, leaving the motor home for LaVonne and Stefan to sell.

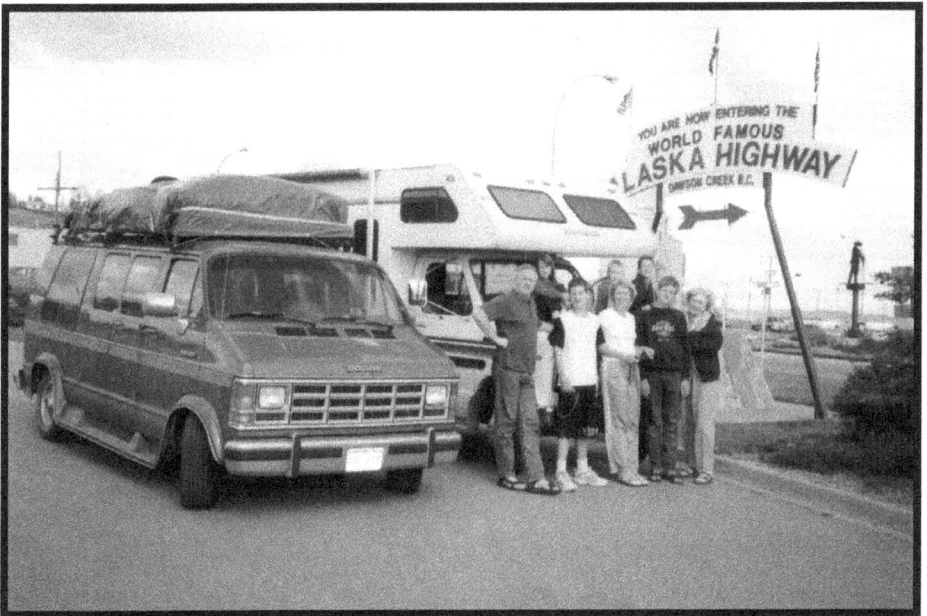

Looking through pictures from that trip, and talking about the memories made us realize how much fun we had traveling in a motor home. We were looking for a new one when Orla's brother-in-law called to say he was selling his big, fancy motor home, with one slide, hardwood flooring and wall-to-wall carpeting, fully equipped kitchen, laundry room, and a comfortable bedroom and bathroom. Our first trip in our new motor home was to California to visit old friends. We were staying in a campground in Temecula and the rains came tumbling down.

It never rains in California
But girl let me warn you
It pours, man it pours.

I have always loved the sound of rain, but have never been able to really enjoy it, as we were always worried that, somewhere, one of the properties would have a leaky roof. Now, all of the properties sold and gone, we sat in our motor home and listened to the rain on the roof, and it was so wonderful to just relax and enjoy it.

In 2005 my nephew from Sweden was getting married in North Carolina. We decided to take the motor home to the wedding, stopping at places along the way and making an adventure of the trip. We had been to Branson, Missouri once before and, since it was on the way, planned to stop there for a week and see a few shows. My sister, Solveig, was traveling with us. In Branson we joked that she should buy a house and, just for fun, we booked an appointment with a real estate agent.

She showed us several properties; one was a country style house with a beautiful front porch on a nice quiet street. We weren't really shopping though, only looking. Leaving Branson Solveig kept talking about how nice that house was, so nicely decorated; beautiful kitchen, and the bathtub had a handle to make it easier to climb in and out. After a day of talking about it Orla said, "Let's buy it!"

By the time we reached North Carolina our offer was accepted.

Calling LaVonne, I said, "You'll never guess what we did on our vacation!"

"You bought a house."

How could she know that I wondered?

"That's what you guys do," she answered.

I really love Branson. I love sitting on our front porch in the

morning, waving to the neighbors as they leave for work. We have such wonderful neighbors. Flowers grow better in Branson than they do in Colorado and I have always loved having flowers around me. But our son Orla Jens, his wife, Darla, and their two little girls, Lydia and Mallory, live in Colorado Springs and so do many of our friends. We don't want to leave. So now we divide our time between our home in Colorado Springs and our home in Branson. The best of two worlds.

People I've Met

My Parents

My parents, of course, influenced me both positively and negatively.

My father was always a man of his word. If he told me something, I knew I could count on it. On the other hand he was not very good at communicating.

My mother was so loving and gentle, even when she was sick and suffering. Losing her has left a terrible scar, one I have lived with all my life, that won't completely heal until I see her again in heaven.

Pastor Eidersjö

Pastor Eidersjö and his family, who in my eyes were the ideal family, were very loving and caring. They had a daughter, Viola, who was my age, and a son, Lennart, who was four years younger. We were always welcome when we came to visit, and they would often hold a Bible study. Pastor Eidersjö was the pastor at the time of the revival when both my parents were saved. Many, many years later, Linnea and I went to see him when he was in a nursing home in Gränna. Ninety years old, with his sense of humor was still intact, he was sitting in a chair wearing an Arab headdress. He said he was wearing it to scare the nurses. Linnea told him we had come to visit so that he could "see a part of his harvest," meaning that we were the result of the spiritual seeds he had sown.

Saliga Emma.

I was 12 years old when Saliga Emma celebrated her 75th birthday. I remember her well. She was very faithful, and I thank the Lord for Emma who was obedient to the call.

Had she not been obedient there would not be a chapel.

If there were no chapel, Pastor Ejdersjö would not have come.

If Pastor Eidersjö had not come, there might not have been a revival.

If there had not been a revival my parents may not have been saved.

If my parents had not been saved, where would I be?

How important it is that we are obedient to His call and are faithful in prayer.

The Dobsons

Dr. James and Shirley Dobson lived in Arcadia and attended the same church we did. Many times Shirley would invite us to come and sit with them, and included us at their parties. She warmed my heart with her hospitality and sense of humor. There have been many times when I have been encouraged by their friendship and, of course, their books. We invited them over to dinner one day and asked Jim to say the blessing. He prayed beautifully, thanking the Lord for the fleeting moments of our lives. I remember thinking that life isn't that short. Today I realize that he was right, life is but a fleeting moment. Orla Jens is the same age as their daughter, Danae, and spent a lot of time at their home. They were a great influence on him and he could talk to them about things he had trouble talking to us about. One evening he came home late. When I asked him where he had been he said he'd been at the Dobsons. Well, then it was ok. If that's where he spent his time I wouldn't worry.

There are so many more that have influenced me and shaped my life. Dear friends like Ken and Carol Norheim, and David and Jeanette Crocker have been an inspiration as their lives have reflected God's grace even through desperate struggles. My prayer partners, Kathy and Katie, have supported me through many dark days, and have granted me the blessing of being able to carry them to Jesus during their times of struggle. My children, all of them including our "bonus children," continue to bless my life with encouragement and inspiration. I can't possibly name all of the dear friends that have meant so much to me. I have named only a few of all the many people I have met or encountered who have changed the course of my life, but I thank God for all of you.

Lessons I've Learned

*T*his has turned into a long story. It has been a journey into a past that now seems so near, the details becoming clearer as I write. My sisters have contributed with their memories, and it has been a joy to involve them in the process, calling them with questions of how things really looked or happened. My life has been long and full of blessings. I have seen more good than evil, more beauty than ugliness, more joy than sorrow. It has been a good life.

I've learned that touching someone's life is more important than building monuments.

My father worked hard on his farm, clearing the fields and taking care of the forest. His dream was that the seven of us would share ownership of the farm, and once a year we could all gather, bringing our families for a big party. He visualized

lots of grandchildren running over the fields, climbing the trees and fishing in the lake.

When he was older he signed the farm over to all of us to own equally. A few years later, Ove and Yvonne wanted to sell their share, asking us to buy them out, and so we did. Years later Kurt, the baby of the family, got married, and they wanted to buy the farm from the rest of us. They built a beautiful house on the same spot where the old farmhouse once stood, clearing the forest so you can see Göla from the house, and making many improvements to the farm. It was exciting to see the farm come alive again, but then Kurt and Ylva decided to divorce. The property was divided, Kurt getting the forest and Ylva taking the buildings and fields. She recently sold her portion to Danes, and so my father's farm is now in the hands of strangers.

We have had some parties in Lindö but never with all seven of us at the same time. Solveig, Ove, and I all immigrated to the states. Ove has never been back. In 2000 we had a sibling reunion in Colorado Springs. For the first time in 48 years, we were all united.

Sometimes we drive past properties we have owned in the past, properties I worked hard to beautify, painting inside and out, planting flowers and trees, and fighting the dirt, weeds and vandalism. Today, these properties, like my father's farm, belong to strangers. Some of them have been terribly neglected; the trees and shrubs I planted have long since died.

[A man] heaps up wealth, not knowing who will get it.
Psalms 39:6

Long after I am gone, the properties and belongings that I have had will also most likely be gone, but the people I have been privileged to touch and to witness to will, in their turn, witness to others, and the legacy will continue.

I have learned that despite my failures, God works His purpose in my life and in the lives of those around me.

Our daughter, LaVonne, was enrolled in the nursing program at Point Loma College in San Diego. All her life I had encouraged her, and influenced her, towards this goal to go to college, and to study nursing. I felt that nursing was a good career, something I had wanted to pursue myself, but had instead chosen a different path. Compliant as always, she followed my advice. I never realized that she didn't really like nursing. I regret that I misguided her.

In 1980 we were visiting in Sweden over the summer. While attending a camp on Elida, a gospel sailing vessel on Sweden's west coast, LaVonne met and fell in love with Stefan. Their romance continued even after she came home and returned to school, with phone calls and letters frequently crossing the ocean. Stefan was already producing films at that time, and had his own production company. In April he came to California with a small team. He stayed for six months working on several different projects. When he came again at Christmas we understood that their relationship was getting serious.

In January LaVonne told me they wanted to get married. Although my whole being cried out that she was too young, and I was afraid that she would move away from us, the only concern I voiced was that she had to finish school. This she promised to do.

The wedding was set for June 19th. Since LaVonne was still in school most of the planning and organizing fell on me. By the end of May I was beginning to feel worried and anxious. Had I made a terrible mistake allowing this wedding to happen?

In early June the anxiety was tearing me apart. I confessed all of this to my prayer partner, Kathy, and we laid it all before the Lord. I cried out to God, "What should I do?"

An answer came, "Pray for them."

Stefan's father, his two brothers and their wives, and his young nephew were all coming for the wedding. Because of health issues his mother had to stay home. We happened to have a rental house empty at the time, and I furnished it and stocked it with linens and cookware so that they would have a place to stay. We met them for the first time when they arrived in California two weeks before the wedding. They were, and are, very nice people. Peter, one of Stefan's brothers, and his wife were going to sing at the wedding and Stefan's three-year-old nephew was going to be the ring bearer. He was so cute in his tiny tuxedo.

The rehearsal dinner was held in our backyard. Our dear friends, David and Jeanette, helped me with all the arrangements, setting up tables and serving the food. It was a beautiful California evening.

On the morning of the wedding I fell on my knees and begged God to help me not to cry and spoil the wedding. It was a beautiful wedding with lots of flowers, candles and music. Pastor Lee, from the Nazarene Church, and Dr. Sam Kameleson, a dear friend, both officiated. LaVonne wanted the ceremony to glorify God and I think we succeeded in that. Young and graceful, she was a beautiful bride with Stefan as her handsome prince. At the reception following we served a Swedish smorgasbord. Everything went as planned. The bride and groom were happy, the guests were all pleased and I didn't cry. But when it was all over I cried like I had never cried before.

After the wedding I fell into a deep depression. I mourned the passing of time, obsessed over perceived mistakes, and despaired for the future. Although I still functioned and kept control of my business, my family and closest friends noticed that I was depressed.

LaVonne and Stefan returned from their extended honeymoon in Sweden. They found an apartment in Arcadia and she transferred to Azusa Pacific College to finish her senior year. Stefan worked for a short time with a Christian film company, and then looked for any work he could find, painting, gardening, and even roofing. In the spring he went back to Sweden to take care of business and then to Sri Lanka on a film project. As a new bride, in a new home, attending a new school with all the pressures of studying, seeing me struggle through depression added another burden on LaVonne's young shoulders, but she never gave up. She graduated on time and later took and passed her boards, receiving her R.N.

I'd heard people talk of depression and being depressed, but I never understood what it meant to be depressed. I felt as if I were in a long, dark tunnel, with no end in sight. Looking through my journal I can see how God was walking with me in the tunnel.

November 29,1982 – Many dark days have passed and today is yet another one. However, I got a word from the Lord. "A little more than a year you shall be shaken by anxiety." That is what I read today. I wonder what it means.

December 3 – I got another Rhema from God. "Before I formed you in your mother's womb I knew you. And before you were born I consecrated you."

December 12 – As I was waking up I heard a still, small voice saying, "You might as well be happy."

One day I received a message, "Let go of what you have in your hands so I can bless you."

Another day the message was about forgiveness. "You must forgive yourself as well as others."

God is good; He never left my side. My depression lasted about a year, and as I walked out of that tunnel and into the light, I began to see God's purpose. I now have a new understanding and compassion for people with mental illnesses, specifically depression.

Today LaVonne and Stefan are prospering; their marriage is strong, and they have given us five blessed grandchildren that have brought music, laughter and joy into my life. Although they live far away in Sweden our relationship has healed and is now strong. She is no longer nursing. Today she works with her husband in their production company, producing documentaries for television and a DVD home market. Lately she has begun to hone her writing skills, discovering a talent that has long lain dormant, and her artistic vein has found expression in layout and design.

We know that in all things
God works for the good of those who love him,
who have been called according to his purpose.
Romans 8:28

Sometimes I failed greatly, made the wrong decision, did the wrong thing, or uttered hurtful words. There are many regrets. I am flawed, but not rejected. Jesus is the potter, and I am the clay, He didn't throw me away when I turned out differently than He had planned, but continued to mold me and use me. Praise God!

I have learned that God cares about me personally and intercedes in my life to carry me through the darkest of days.

Throughout my life I have witnessed the goodness of God and the power of his hand in our lives. Of course there have been times in my life when I've wondered where God was or why he didn't intercede, but even during those two years when I struggled through a depression I felt His presence, received guidance and comfort during those dark days. I've seen lives changed when faith entered, experienced healing in both body and relationships, and felt a strength that carries through great sorrow.

Birgitta and Erik live in a small town in Sweden where they raised six children. Both are wonderful Christians. As a family they prayed together and played together. Birgitta told me that when they were all asleep she would walk around to each bed and pray over them. You would think that nothing bad would ever happen to them.

One evening when Erik came home from work he found his 16 year old son, Olle, had killed himself. When Birgitta came home she was shocked to see an ambulance in front of the house.

Their very good friends from the church came over immediately, and wisely decided that they needed to take the family away from the scene. They went to Småland to Erik's niece and stayed there a few days, trying to keep busy. That was the best thing they could have done for them.

In the mean time other friends came in and took care of everything so the house would look as pleasant as possible when they came back. Only there was no Olle.

With the help of friends they got through the funeral. Erik said to Birgitta, "Life must go on."

Birgitta answered in disbelief, "Will it?"

They were both filled with sorrow, anxiety and questions. Where is God? And where might Olle be now? Did he go to Heaven or to hell?

About two months later they decided to visit a large church in Arvika about 40 miles from home. With heavy hearts they tried to take part in the worship, but they didn't really feel like it.

When the preacher started to preach he suddenly stopped for a minute and said, "I got a message from the Lord to someone. You are a mother who is here full of anxiety and sadness. You have lost a son and you are worried about where he is. The Lord says you don't have worry about him for your son is home with me in heaven."

How great is our God? He is too great for me to understand everything but small enough to communicate on our level and let us know how much He cares for us.

I have included this story with Birgitta's permission, only to tell you what a magnificent God we have.

Those who know your name will trust in you, for you, LORD, have never forsaken those who seek you.
Psalm 9:10

In 2000 we were planning a sibling reunion. The last time we had all been together was in 1953, just before my first trip to the United States. Three of us were now living in the USA; Solveig in California, Ove in Montana, and I in Colorado. Linnea, Birgitta, Yvonne and Kurt were still living in Sweden. In the fall we planned to unite again, in Colorado. We were looking forward to being together but our plans were threatened by two tragic and sudden losses in the family.

In March my sister Solveig's husband, Carl, died suddenly from an aortic aneurism. He was a train conductor and trains were his passion. Carl was working when he collapsed, dying almost instantly. At 61 he was looking forward to retirement when he and Solveig would be able to travel and pursue his great interest in trains. Carl's death came as a great shock and we miss him terribly.

Two months later my niece, Linnea's daughter, Else-Marie, died suddenly from a blood clot in her leg that went to her heart. She was only 49 years old, and left behind her husband and four sons, the youngest still in his teens. Linnea was nearly paralyzed with grief. She had enjoyed a special relationship with her daughter and the two women were best friends as well as mother and daughter.

I really doubted that after these two tragedies we would be able to hold our reunion as planned. But when I went to Sweden for Else-Marie's funeral, Linnea's son, Roger, encouraged me to continue with the plans and do everything in my power to get Linnea to come. She really needed a change of scenery and something that could lift her spirits.

I spent a lot of time in prayer that summer, praying for my two sisters who had sustained such loss, praying that they would find the strength to attend our reunion, and that the rest of my siblings would also attend. God is so good. When things seem impossible He works behind the scenes. Everything just seemed to come together. Solveig arrived from California, my brother, Ove, came from Montana, and Linnea, Birgitta, Yvonne and Kurt all came from Sweden. We had such a good and blessed time together and I think my dear sisters began to heal.

Reunited after 47 years. From left: Kurt, Ove, Solveig, May-Britt, Linnea, Birgitta, Ywonne

> *Because of the Lord's great love*
> *we are not consumed,*
> *for his compassions never fail.*
> *They are new every morning;*
> *great is your faithfulness.*
> *Lamentations 3:22-23*

I have known many glorious days when I've praised God for his goodness, but it's been during those dark days of tribulation when I've experienced just how much He loves me and how He has carried me through the hard times. His mercies are new every morning. GREAT is His faithfulness!

My greatest joy has been raising my children. I enjoyed every moment. Looking back I wish I had not worked so hard, but had instead, spent more time with them. The moments were so fleeting.

My greatest triumphs have been seeing the people I have loved and prayed for come to the Lord. I am so grateful to God that he chose me to be an influence in their lives.

The greatest lessons I have learned is to savor each day. They pass so quickly. It seems only a moment has past since I was a child, and in only moments it will be over.

> *Yesterday is gone*
> *Tomorrow may never come*
> *But we have this moment today**

---

*"We Have This Moment, Today"
William J. Gaither, Gloria Gaither
© 1975 Gaither Music Company (ASCAP)
All rights controlled by Gaither Copyright Management
Used by permission

Do you know Jesus?

If you don't I would like to encourage and admonish you to receive Him as your personal Savior. He has been my friend most of my life and I have always felt I had someone to talk to. It does not mean that you will never have any problems or setbacks, but it means you will always have someone to share your burdens.

For God so loved the world
that he gave his one and only Son,
that whoever believes in him
shall not perish but have eternal life.
John 3:16

Prayer for salvation:

Dear God I believe that you are God and I believe that you sent your son, Jesus Christ, to die for my sins.

I confess that I am a sinner and I ask you to forgive my sins. I ask you to be my Savior and my Lord.

Fill me with your Holy Spirit according to your promise and guide me through life.

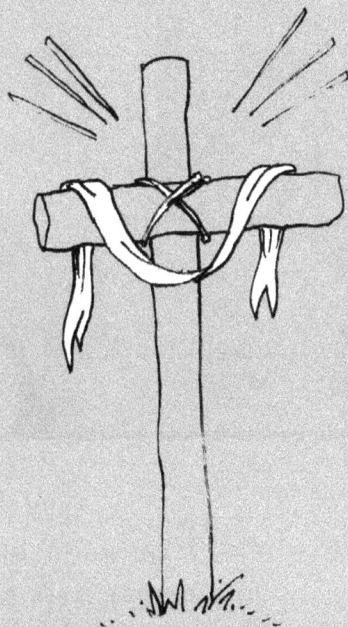

The Rest of the Story

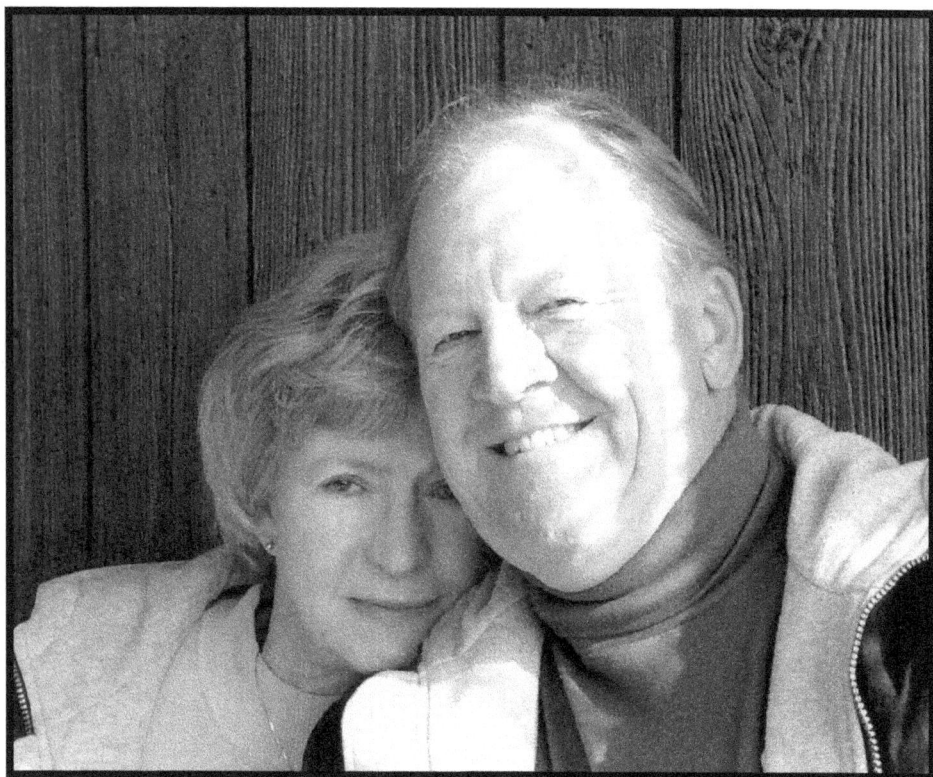

This year I celebrate 50 years of marriage to a man who has been my lover, my partner, my friend. I have treasured these years together, and look forward to as many more as God will give us.

To my children and grandchildren I say, "Be there! When the time comes I will be waiting on the other side of the gate."

Whether you turn to the right or to the left,
your ears will hear a voice behind you, saying,
"This is the way, walk in it."
Isaiah 30:21

STAY CLOSE TO THE LORD
AND KEEP LISTENING!

Now to Him who is able to keep us from falling
and will present us before His glorious presence
without fault and with great joy
– to the only God our Savior
be glory, majesty, power and authority
through Jesus Christ our Lord,
before all ages, now and forever more! Amen
Jude 1:24

Thanks to God for my redeemer
Thanks for all that you provide
Thanks for times now but a memory
Thanks for Jesus by my side

Thanks for pleasant, balmy springtime
Thanks for dark and dreary fall
Thanks for tears by now forgotten
Thanks for peace within my soul

Thanks for prayers you have answered
Thanks for what you have denied
Thanks for storms that I have weathered
Thanks for all you have supplied

Thanks for pain and thanks for pleasure
Thanks for comfort in despair
Thanks for grace that none can measure
Thanks for love beyond compare

Thanks for roses by the wayside
Thanks for thorns their stems contain
Thanks for home and thanks for fireside
Thanks for hope, that sweet refrain

Thanks for joy and thanks for sorrow
Thanks for heavenly peace with you
Thanks for hope in the tomorrow
Thanks for all eternity

---

*I would like this song sung at my funeral
"Thanks to God for My Redeemer"
original Swedish "Tack O Gud"
August Ludwig Storm - 1891
Translation: Carl E. Backstrom - 1910

www.ingramcontent.com/pod-product-compliance
Lightning Source LLC
Chambersburg PA
CBHW031833090426
42741CB00005B/224